AMAZON SPEAKS
Stories
for the Spirit

Also by Connie Grauds

Jungle Medicine: From Medicine to Magic
A spirited tale of transformation in the Amazon.

The Energy Prescription:
Give Yourself Abundant Vitality with the Wisdom
of America's Leading Natural Pharmacist
with co-author Doug Childers
The answer to the energy crisis within.

AMAZON SPEAKS

Stories
for the Spirit

Connie Grauds

THE CENTER FOR SPIRITED MEDICINE

Amazon Speaks: Stories for the Spirit

ISBN-10: 0974730319
ISBN-13: 978-0974730318

1. Grauds, Connie 2. Shamanism--Amazon River Valley
3. Iquitos, Peru 4. Ecological Medicine 5. Pharmacists--
United States--Biography

Book design by Susan Pomeroy
Editing by Michelle Kalman

Published by
The Center for Spirited Medicine

There Is a River

There is a river in my heart,
a river in my eyes,
my memory, my touch.

The river lives in all of us,
especially when
we close the eyes
and know it from <u>inside</u>.

How does the river know
which way to turn,
which fish to loose into the nets
and which to direct around?

The river moves slowly here
in my heart—slower
even than the heartbeat
and I can see its rhythm
in the waves moving toward shore,
toward a home for all waves.

This river is an angel
calling us, calling and calling
like a mother for her young,
and we answer with our longing
to swim in this wet place
downstream, again and again.

What is this river
if not a mouth
speaking in its own way,
speaking like the wolf,
like the eagle, like the bear.

This river spins its way
into the current that pulls,
pulls us under,
down, down and down,
into the depths
and what we don't know.

So river...
When do you speak
in that clear voice
gods and poets

have talked about?
They made it look easy,
this calling a river.

But you won't be easy.
You will call me out
again and again—asking
for the truth and knowing
there are many versions.

Maybe you are the river
in my heart to guide me,
or maybe simply to flow
like the wind has
in the past.

Whatever—you will call
or you will flow
and some day I will hear you
with new ears.

Amazon Poet

Table of Contents

Author's Note: Stories may be read in any order.

Preface
Love of Life

Long ago in a far-away place, yet near and dear to my heart, I walked for the first time through the shimmering Emerald Doors of the Amazon—the greatest expression of life on Earth. My life has never been the same.

After almost 25 years of apprenticeship in Amazonian shamanism in the jungles of Peru—the spirited tales of which are recounted in my book *Jungle Medicine*—I bring to you more stories for your own continuing personal apprenticeship to spirit.

As a shamana, my role is to heal the sick and honor the forest. My duty is to look after the well-being of both man and Mother Nature.

Traditionally trained, I not only keep my obligations as healer and keeper of the ancient ways, but also lead efforts in respect for and conservation of Nature in the largest sense.

I take responsible action, and urge others to do so also, for the protection of the forest, the ecosystem that supports the Earth and all its inhabitants. This is where the rubber hits the road—or where the paddle hits the river, as we say in the Amazon.

The Amazon River basin covers some 40% of the South American continent. It is home to the largest rainforest on Earth, and home to one-fifth of the plant and animal species on Earth. The Amazon rainforest covers an area nearly equal to the size of the contiguous 48 U.S. states. The Amazon River itself is the most voluminous river on Earth, eleven times the volume of the Mississippi. The river's mouth may be 300 miles wide during high water season. All this is where the power lies.

The Amazon is both the Beauty and the Beast. She is an incredible force to be reckoned with indeed. She will lift your spirits with her eye-dazzling beauty of neon-colored flora and fauna, urging the viewer to *pay attention* to the greatest giver of life on Earth. And, she is also the Wild Feminine. No one tames the wild tempestuous beast of the Amazon. All are best advised to learn by the ebb and flow of her tempers and ways. Anyone who courts the spirit of the Amazon will surely be smitten, as have I.

To state it simply, in the Amazon, we are brought home again. Upon his first deep nature visit with me to the Amazon, a business executive friend of mine said, "I feel at home here, and I really don't know why."

To paraphrase Carl Gustav Jung: Perhaps we should be scientific—or perhaps we should be poetic and idyllic about nature. The truth about nature needs scientific expression, it needs spiritual expression, and it needs artistic expression. It needs the poet and the musician. And even then you only express part of it.

Here are more than twenty randomly-ordered vignettes, the many voices of the spirit of the Amazon, from the sacred to the profane. Some stories will transport you to the Amazon jungle, others will rivet you where you now sit. Still others will shift your consciousness. There are stories of spirit to lift your heart; there are facts of science that sober the spirit. May you deepen your respect and passion for her Nature. I believe that as you learn from her wisdom and love her, you may be called to take action to defend her, support her, and to see her flourish—for in great Love, there is Life itself.

Connie Grauds
Amazon jungles of Iquitos, Peru
September 28, 2017

1
Why Do
Old People Shake?

Insecurities. We all have them. But I often
wonder, why do we have them and what purpose
do they serve? Is self-doubt merely a lack of faith
or confidence in oneself? Or, is it also just
another excuse to not do something, not
take responsibility.

It is the end of yet another inspiring day in
the heart of the Amazon jungles of Peru.
Even after almost 25 years of the Amazon as my

second home, just when I'm lulled into thinking there are no more ways in which the Amazon could possibly dazzle me, I am awe-struck once again—this time by a perfectly complete rainbow, arching over the Amazon Heliconia Lodge, as the boat pulls up to the mud-soaked dock area. All the lodge guests excitedly point to this magnificent and colorful *arco iris*, the arch-of-the-iris rainbow, heaven sent from the gods of the Amazon. We regularly see lots of rainbows in the Amazon, as it rains some two out of three days a year or more. Yet today I see the rainbow anew, with my soul, as a sign of hope and perfection, uniting the Heavens and the Earth—a sign that all's well in this Garden of Eden.

The lodge guests and I all single-file off the boat, then from the dock up the crooked wooden steps, and then trample through the cool of the open reception area to the screened-in dining room. On land, at last. Hot and sweaty from the hours of our boat ride excursion up the river, we line up for the welcoming thirst-quenching libations. Peering over the tops of our glasses of *limonada*, we are mesmerized by the mostly gray and sometimes pink fresh-water river dolphins excitedly leaping out of the water again and again to feast on the late day's many schools of fish.

Those with *limonada* begin taking seats at the tables, many wipe hot humid trickles from their faces and most eagerly share dolphin-sighting stories. The last of the guests to go through the welcoming-drink line ahead of me are a family from San Francisco, California— mom, dad and their precocious four-year-old boy. As they find their way to some empty seats, the little boy stares at me for a few minutes and then turns to his parents and blurts out with his big-boy voice for all to hear, "Why do old people shake?"

There is dead silence at the table. I am mortified. My doctors have told me that I have familial benign essential tremors in my neck. In other words, I have the Katherine Hepburn tremor-syndrome.

I am shocked that my secret, which is obvious for everyone to see, is talked about so openly—more than I have ever been able to do. I take an empty seat next to my *maestro* of nearly 25 years—one of the last of the Amazon jungle shamans—to calm myself. I find my composure in drinking my *limonada*. My *maestro* asks what just happened, as he could feel the energy shift of the room a few moments earlier.

Upon hearing the explanation, the shaman comments, "You're not old. Some may think that you may be old in years, but not old in spirit. You simply have much good energy, *mucha energia positiva*, running through your body. When it hits the arthritis in your neck, it causes the shake. It's a good thing, Connie. You should be proud that you've worked so hard in your 25 years of shamanic apprenticeship to now have so much good energy that it shows!"

But I don't feel good. I am still wracked with insecurity, and overly self-absorbed in the moment. Is the whole world staring at me because of this benign human condition? I desperately stare into my *maestro's* exotic brown sun-weathered face for answers.

My *maestro* replies with shocking enthusiasm, "I hope they are staring at you! The spirits have given you lots to say, and now people will pay attention to you. Get on with your work in the world. Let the spirits dance in your body as they will."

2
They Came to Laugh

When the student is ready the teacher will appear. This is a truism we've all heard. My lesson came instead as "when the student is ready the teacher will *disappear*."

It is a trip much like any one of a number of trips per year that I take into the Amazon jungles of Peru. I am due to arrive into Iquitos in October to meet up with my *maestro,* and together go by boat to visit the village of Jaldar on the Yarapa River.

I have never been to the indigenous village of Jaldar, and neither has my *maestro*. We have been invited by a jungle-lover acquaintance of mine, Krys, who is a neighbor in Marin, California. She has built a jungle *tambo* house in Jaldar some years ago that she visits regularly.

Krys has traveled to Jaldar ahead of me to set up the house in anticipation of my arrival. It turns out that only I will be visiting Jaldar, as my *maestro* was called away from Iquitos last-minute to work in another village down river.

Today is the day before I leave Iquitos to travel to Jaldar, I must alert Krys to let her know I'll be arriving and at what time, so she can arrange for a small boat to pick me up from the main river to ferry me to Jaldar. As there are no phones in Jaldar to call ahead, she has instructed me on how best to contact her. I go to the local radio station *Voz de la Selva*, Voice of the Jungle, in Iquitos. There, I join a long line of people waiting to get their messages out. Finally, it's my turn. I pay the radio broadcaster one *sol*—about 25 cents, going exchange rate—

and place my request. He then announces over the radio that I will be arriving tomorrow at Puerto Miguel—the port that I must get off at, to then catch my small private boat to Jaldar—sometime after midnight, most likely closer to 2am.

Apparently, there is a central radio receiving station in Jaldar in the public square, that blasts out over a large external speaker a stream of continuous announcements and messages of one kind or another—including mine. I trust somebody in the village will hear the message and relay it to Krys. An ingenious system—a sort of techno-jungle-drum.

My departure day has arrived. As I step onto a large *colectivo*, public boat taxi, in Iquitos, I am immediately overwhelmed by the pushing and shoving of passengers, produce, animals, and boat workers. As if the jungle itself isn't sweltering and humid enough, I am crammed so close to my fellow passengers that I'm over-taken by the smell of their hot breath and can almost taste the spicy lunch they downed before boarding.

Nervously watching several large black furry tarantulas navigating over the mountains and valleys of green banana bunches, I quickly decide to solicit a boat worker to find me a private space where I can hide from the overwhelm of the smell and crush of humanity, the flapping of chickens and fish, and the sweet-sour odors of overly ripe jungle fruits and vegetables.

The so-called private berth that I pay good money for turns out to be nothing more than a 4x4x4 cubicle. Making the most of it, I decide to sit cross-legged and push myself deep into the cubicle to avoid as much of the chaos as possible. The tiny cubicle is hot with no cross-breeze for relief, and I begin to wonder how I will manage to endure the next five long hours of slow boat ride ahead.

It's now dark outside. The sun sets just before 6pm every day of the year, as this part of the Amazon is near the equator. Five long dark hours lie ahead. After an hour of listening to the incessant drone of the hard-working rusty engines that push the passengers and cargo to their destinations, I ask myself, "Where am I?" It begins to dawn on me that no one knows where I am. My mind and my fears start to work overtime. If I were to fall overboard, my mind convinces me, hordes of caiman would feast on my sweet white flesh. No *maestro* to comfort me. Born more than three-quarters of a century ago deep in the Amazon jungles of Peru, he knows how to survive, live and thrive here. I always feel safe around him. Now I beg the gods of the Amazon to be with me, as I'm left to call upon my own skills and intuition.

It's after midnight as we approach the village of Puerto Miguel where I am to disembark. It begins to rain. A friend informed me earlier that because it is the low-water time of the year and portage would be necessary, there would be young men waiting at Puerto Miguel that I could hire to portage my baggage across a small land mass. This portage would get me to the Yarapa River where a private boat would be waiting for me. I am either a fool to have believed that story, or the jungle has its own wisdom that defies the western mind. I pray it's the latter.

I pay a few *soles* to a questionable-looking skinny teenage porter, but to my surprise he has the strength of an ox. In no time flat, he's run-walking down the path balancing my luggage on his back with me in tow covered by my green plastic poncho. I have no idea how far or how long this portage hike will be. A rivulet of hot sweat is trickling down my cleavage under my rain poncho, in the steamy nighttime jungle heat. More sweat, fueled by my increasing fear, trickles past my ears. The rains turn torrential.

Miraculously we finally reach the Yarapa River in one soggy piece with my rain-soaked luggage in tow. I am so glad to see the dug-out canoe and my Jaldar village connection, Alejandro, waiting for me in the pouring rain. There is no time for the niceties of introductions, as the jungle storm commands our attention. I step into the dug-out, Alejandro starts the *peque-peque*, a small putt-putt boat motor. However slow it's putt-putting along, I'm grateful that Alejandro did not hand me a paddle.

The winds are adding to the raging orchestral thunder-and-lightning storm, a *tormenta*. The rain is pummeling us at a forty-five degree angle as we motor on in this hand-hewn dug-out with no protective canopy. Some twenty minutes later, I look down to check my rain-soaked shoes when I realize that the boat is filling with water and seems about to capsize. I holler at Alejandro to get his attention—he, too, is now aware of our dire situation. Io my surprise, Alejandro turns off the motor and jumps overboard to lighten the load of the boat so it can float. Grabbing the rope at the front of the boat, he swims with all his might to man-power the boat to shore. At last, we unceremoniously arrive at the small indigenous village of Jaldar. Whew!

Anxious to be on solid ground, I quickly scramble off the boat, thanking every god of the Amazon for my life. Human forms come out of the black night to join us down at the shore and help me unload into the *tambo*, the thatched roof village house, where I will stay for the next week.

The storm has subsided. It's almost 3am. Krys gives me a welcoming hug, and offers to translate my introduction into Spanish. I introduce myself briefly, given the early morning hours and the rain-soaked state of our tiredness. Keeping it short, I mention that I am a pharmacist by education, with a huge interest in natural medicines. I apologize that my *maestro* will not be with us, and conclude by stating that I have apprenticed with him for over a decade.

From the expressions on their faces, I immediately realize that to the villagers my college education is unimportant. What they really want from me, or anyone they meet, is to experience and know me in their hearts. My heart opens, and spontaneously I suggest that I would be more than happy to give all of them a shamanic energy blessing in gratitude for their warm welcome and all their assistance in getting me ashore.

"Come to the river's edge at sundown tomorrow," I suggest, "and we'll do a blessing ritual." All five nod their heads and smile. With that agreement, we each head our separate ways to get some rest.

In my room, I shake the raindrops from my poncho, but can't shake the idea that I had just overstepped my bounds somehow. My *maestro* is always the one who gives this blessing ritual. Who am I, the mere apprentice, to think that I am capable of giving a traditional Amazonian blessing ritual to a bunch of Amazonians? Too tired to think about it any further, I crawl under my mosquito netting into bed for the few remaining hours of night.

The next afternoon, I explore the village and surrounds. Just before dusk, I discover a group of tree stumps forming a circle, and decide this is to be the location of the ritual. There were five who helped me from the boat and to my room yesterday and there are nine tree stumps, plenty of seats for everyone. Lighting kerosene lamps at sunset to create the sacred circle space, the five invited people easily find their way in the dark to this designated location.

As they each take a seat, I glance up to see a curious trail of lit torches heading my way. Soon there are ten more people joining our ritual circle. Obviously, the jungle drums have spread the gossip of the evening ritual. With big smiles on their faces, I readily welcome them all with open arms and an open heart.

I invite one of the men standing to take a seat on the main tree stump in the center of the circle. He is to be the first to receive a blessing. I gather myself and call in spirit, with the realization that the only thing I can do in my *maestro's* absence is to mimic what he does and hope it works.

The first blessing goes well enough. I ask the next man standing to take a tree stump seat in the center circle and repeat the ritual process. As I finish up, I say *servido*, you've been served, and motion for him to get up and take his seat around the circle. He does not move. Thinking that he didn't hear me or didn't understand my

Spanish, I repeat *servido* again in a louder voice and take his hand, motioning for him to stand up and go. With some prodding, he finally comes out of what seems like a bit of confusion and moves on to take his seat outside of the center.

I notice the energy shift in the evening air, as the spirit of my *mapacho*, local tobacco, cigarette begins to take over me, shifting my consciousness and the energy of the group of participants.

The third man to receive a blessing now takes the center tree stump seat and receives his blessing. *Servido*, I say, you've been served. But he doesn't move. Louder I say *servido*, but still no movement from the stump. Reaching down I take his right hand to urge him toward his seat. No movement, but his right arm stays strangely outstretched in mid-air. Puzzled, I take his left hand and gently pull his left arm up and forward. Still no movement, but now both arms are reaching skyward. I'm beginning to wonder if the villagers are playing a game on me, something like "stump the shaman". With piqued curiosity, I bend over to look into the man's face. To my surprise, I see that his eyes are rolled back into his head. He is in a trance, his arms reaching to the heavens above in ecstatic rapture. Now I realize the previous man was in the same trance. *Oh my God—it's working*, I exclaim with wonder, under my breath.

An hour-and-a-half later, the spirit in the air is palpable everywhere and within everyone. I'm finishing with the last of many to receive a blessing. An older woman, maybe about 65 years old judging from the droop of her sagging breasts, steps up to the stump. She is wearing a tee-shirt that says in English "Fabulous after Fifty". I smile, thinking to myself, "If she only knew...."

Her blessing finished, she rises from the tree stump and turns to give me a hug. "Felicita is my name, and I am the village matriarch," she whispers in my ear. Then smiling ear to ear, she says in a loud voice for all to hear, "You *are* a shamana. You are welcome here anytime."

Wow, I humbly think to myself, what an honor and acceptance by the village matriarch herself. Simultaneously, the little hesitating voice in the back of my head wonders what my *maestro* will say about these events that have just transpired.

Kerosene lamps in hand, we all head down our respective jungle paths to get a late bite to eat and then to fall into deep sleep. The village is at peace.

Awakening at sunrise, a time of much bird chatter and cooler temperatures, I smell the coffee brewing on the wood fire stove and know that the others in the house are already up. I crawl from under my mosquito netting and glance through my open door to see what the day's weather will be like. I see three adults squatting outside my door, apparently waiting for me for some reason. I have no idea what they want. Since my Spanish is limited, I motion for them to follow me to the main house where we can find Krys to translate.

Curiously, about a dozen little kids also follow me, single file, to the main house. I wonder if I am just a curiosity, an oddity? Certainly they've seen a *gringa* before. Our motley parade reaches the house, each falling out of rank to take a seat or sit on the floor.

One by one, each villager explains that they have come to me as a shamana to cure their physical ailments. One young man with a bad *machete* wound, another young girl with fever, and an old man with stomach problems. As I listen to each of their plights, my mind tells me that I'm in way over my head. It's one thing to give last night's ritual blessing to bring good spirits, it's quite another to in fact treat these people for physical ailments. I'm no doctor. Yet the look in their eyes tells me that I am their only hope for relief. Their old village shaman died many years ago. They have no means to go by boat to the nearest town of Nauta, some four hours away by paddle canoe, and no money to see a doctor if they finally get there.

My heart goes out to them as I realize that maybe I can be of some help. As any pharmacist traveling, my first-aid kit is packed with three different oral antibiotics and a couple of antibiotic first-aid creams. I also have a jungle medicinal plant remedy book written in Spanish that will come in handy. Step up to the plate, I tell myself. Do what you can for these people, you're more help than they've got right now. Do the best you can for them, it's the right thing to do.

Treating them with what little I have, I make suggestions of some local-growing herbs that might be helpful. A half-hour later, their relatives come to take them home. They all leave happy that help and relief are at hand.

I arise from my wooden stool, ready to find some of that good coffee I still smell brewing. In the kitchen, the house staff and I pour ourselves a cup of coffee, yet another form of morning ritual to greet the dawn. We start the day again, refreshed and full of good spirit from the evening before. I'm all ears as the house staff eagerly share their experiences of last evening's blessing ritual.

An interesting back story begins to unfold. It seems that when I first arrived and introduced myself to say that I had been apprenticing in Amazonian shamanism, they did not believe me. How could I, as a *gringa*, know their sacred Amazonian rituals? In fact, they now tell me when the gossip of my presence in the village first spread, some of the other villagers came to the blessing ritual last night to laugh at me. I foolishly mistook their grins at the ritual to be smiles of pleasure and excitement. They were in fact smirks of distrust. I am shocked to realize my own naïveté.

Now on our second round of coffee, a few passer-by villagers join in chorus to tell me while they initially came to laugh, they left with trust. Those who experienced the blessings are now believers. But, of course, I had to earn their trust—just as I said to myself upon arrival, they need to experience my heart and spirit for themselves.

Later that afternoon, I stroll down to the river's edge to clear my head of the intensity of the day. Walking past a line of clothes strung up to dry—some of them mine—I wonder if my socks are dry yet on this humid jungle day. I see them hanging at the far end of the clothes line, where Felicita is beginning to take the clothes down.

Pinching my socks on the line, I am surprised to feel that they are already dry. "Felicita, how do you get these clothes, especially the thick socks, dry on such damp days?" I inquire. "I use a mirror to dry clothes, don't you?" Felicita responds quizzically. She picks up the small 6 X 9 inch mirror she has propped up on a log facing the drying clothes. How could this impossibly small mirror do any good, I wonder to myself. "I ask the sun to reflect itself in this mirror to dry the clothes," she explains with confidence. "It works every time," Felicita says as she gathers the last of the dry clothes into a wicker basket. She obviously *believes* that the mirror dries the clothes, and so it is true for her. I smile under my breath—yet another bit of housekeeping 'jungle magic' that I have yet to learn.

A week later, I retrace my river journey back to Iquitos where I am to meet up with my *maestro*. We come together at the Ajary's Restaurant overlooking the Iquitos waterfront, and settle into a plate of ceviche, a cup of *café,* and some good conversation. He is curious about my visit to Jaldar, and a bit jealous of my adventure alone. I begin to recount the story sheepishly, wondering if I had overstepped my bounds in offering the blessing ritual to the villagers.

My *maestro* starts to smile, and upon hearing more, bursts into a giant grin and says, "Congratulations! You're not my student anymore. When people have an experience because of your work and acknowledge the power of your work, then you know you are a shamana."

3
It's Your Turn Now

It's not uncommon to continue an apprentice-ship even after the formal apprenticeship is over. It is a show of respect for one's elders, for experience, lineage, and power greater than one's own.

In my 20th year of apprenticeship, my *maestro* takes me aside from my friends early on a cool Amazon morning. He cups his hands to whisper in my ear, "Will you find another shaman after I die?" A strange question for no reason, I think to myself.

My head sweeps sideways to face him, as I respond, "No of course not. I will continue to talk to you in the heavens." He nods his approval. The moment is broken by luggage wrangling. The conversation is dropped.

We are leaving the jungle border town of Iquitos to head down river into the primal rainforest for a week of welcome relief from the many noisy *motokars*, motorcycle jitneys, that clog the streets of Iquitos.

Arriving at the lodge early in the afternoon, my *maestro* and I enjoy our fried catfish and *yuca* jungle lunch after which we all retire to the hammock house to *siesta* the hot afternoon hours away. I fully intend to get my fair share of "hammock burns" this afternoon, I chuckle to myself silently. As the sun gets low on the horizon, the cooler temps cause us to stir and head for the dining room for a cup of black tea known locally as *té puro*.

After a few refreshing sips, my *maestro* blurts out, "You know, when an apprentice becomes a powerful shaman, the *maestro* and the apprentice must get a divorce—go their separate ways."

I put down my cup of tea to listen closely to his words. Why is he telling me this? How, if at all, is it related to his comment after the Jaldar experience, that I am not his student anymore?

A display of three pink dolphins, the jungle version of Esther Williams' synchronized swimmers, gracefully arch their blunt fins out of the waters of the river and steal our attention away from the conversation.

Jungle nights are a virtual symphony of sounds. The high-pitched piccolo bird tweets, the clarinet section of crickets, and the frogs' low drumbeats begin to warm up after dark. By 8pm, the orchestra is in deafening surround-sound. Some visitors to the jungle are unable to tolerate the intensity and ask to return immediately to Iquitos after their first night. The jungle is not for sissies. To me, the symphony is heavenly and reassuring.

As my *maestro* has taught me, "The healing is in the sights, the smells, and the sounds of the jungle." Nature is "the medicine". As a healer and cancer survivor, I know that unequivocally.

It is bedtime. I fall fast and deep asleep. In my *sueños*, dreams, I see many people gathering around me. Voiceless, they urge me to follow them down the jungle path ahead. I slowly walk forward with the others for about 100 yards. There, the group pulls away to leave me facing alone, the spirit of a woman. She motions for me to walk up the steps ahead, leading the way. Up we go, step by step, for what seems like endless hours of climbing. Confused by where we are headed, with my gut full of fearful tension, the only thing I can do is to continue to follow her.

We finally reach the apex of the never-ending staircase. Ahead of us are two ten-foot-tall closed wooden doors of significance. My eyes bulge in awe at the sight of these gigantic doors. I beg the woman not to open them, for fear of what's on the other side. She does so anyway. A powerful gust of wind and energy swooshes at us as she motions for me to step forward through the doors. As if in some trance state, I automatically follow her directions and step through. Instantly, I find myself out among the stars of the Universe in a sea of black sky. No fear—only bliss.

The next morning, my *maestro* asks if I had any dreams, as he always does daily after breakfast. I recount the dream in every detail. He listens quietly but intently.

When I finish, he looks directly into my eyes and in a sober tone says, "You now have more power than I do. You have reached the top of your struggle to discover your power. Spirit recognized that. My work is done. It's your turn now."

My *maestro* turns his back to me, and takes the path leading into the jungle. Just before he is swallowed up by the ferns, lianas and forest trees, he turns back to me to say, "Remember, Connie, the power of a shaman is known by their work in the world."

His haunting and directive message is carried back to me by the rising early morning mist. I will never forget it.

I believe that it is now our turn, all of us, to step into the powers of our work in the world...may it be so.

4
Raining Tears

Twenty-five years of opening my heart in the Amazon—the Amazon is now in my heart. As a shamana, my obligation is to look after the health and well-being of both man and nature. I'm called to lead efforts in respect for and conservation of Nature. By conservation, I mean con-serve—*"con"* or *with*, and "serve" or *serve with*. Not how do we save "it", but how do we serve "with"—not as if Nature is separate from ourselves. But, how do we recognize and honor that we are *all* Nature. The Amazon is the greatest expression of nature on Earth. Right now, she is in desperate need of our help and conscious attention.

I am staying in an *apartamento* on Avenida La Marina which overlooks the Amazon River. Matching hand-carved rosewood jaguar heads adorn the newel posts at the bottom of the stairs. I climb the wooden spiral staircase leading up to my small "Room With A View", as I call it, cantilevered out over the Amazon River. Leaving the dirt and din of the streets behind, I feel heady as I climb up and up. At last, I'm on top of the world. The 180-degree nature vista surrounding me is breathtaking. The afternoon rain has just finished, and I take my camera to the balcony edge to shoot the gorgeous rainbow left behind. Clicking away, I'm imagining my American friends oohing and aahing over the magnificence of the photos I will email to them.

As I turn off the camera and replace the lens cap, my eyes glance below. At the river's edge I see a good-sized gasoline spill. The gasoline has the same rainbow color pattern reflected on the water as the actual rainbow in the sky—one rainbow deadly, the other life-giving. Styrofoam containers and plastic bottles dot the gasoline-spill rainbow on the water's edge. Limp wet plastic bags are stuck in tree branches from the high-water season. It looks like a prankster is routinely t.p.-ing my front lawn. I spy a bright orange Fanta can intertwined with the overgrowth of green water-lettuce, collecting at the shoreline of the Amazon River below. Decreasing populations of water-lettuce-eating manatees have led to this overgrowth.

It is July 9 and there is a garbage strike going on in all of downtown Iquitos. In my cool of the morning walk through Iquitos, I see the stores, banks, and institutions are all closed. Riot-gear-clad police clutter every street corner and block the through traffic. The town is essentially shut down. Smashed plastic garbage bags spill their stinky contents, littering the streets. An angry crowd is protesting the lack of proper *basura*, garbage, disposal. When it rains today or tomorrow, this unattended garbage will be swept by the gushing rainwater into the sewers, eventually making its way into the river. The sad fact is that the sewers of Iquitos spew their contents into the Mother Amazon.

It's raining. I quickly dart under a small shop canopy while I wrestle to find my poncho. My heart aches. All the rain in the jungles of the Amazon cannot clean away the human sins of insensitivity and carelessness. My consciousness shifts, and I see the great and beautiful Spirit of the Amazon shedding her tears of rain in an attempt to remove the human blight from her skin and veins. *Can you humans hear me crying,* she implores in her saddened eyes. My vision shows me that she is getting tired. Her spirit is dimming. My hand finally reaches the green plastic poncho at the bottom of the damp backpack. My mind returns to normal street consciousness, yet the spirit of the vision remains. I wipe my own tearful eyes with the back of my hand. We must not let her die.

I'm at breakfast the next morning at the Victoria Regia Hotel, a favorite of mine in downtown Iquitos near the Plaza de Armas. On the side table I notice six over-sized picture books of the Amazon region. Perusing them between courses of sweet watermelon and ripe mangos, eggs, fresh soft rolls and tart pineapple juice, I turn my focus from the breathtaking photos of the Amazon to the informative text.

Next to one especially fecund river flora and fauna photo I read that the Amazon River is the world's largest volume river; it contains 20 percent of the fresh water on Earth. This factoid takes hold as I take a sip of fresh clean water from my glass. The Amazon River freshwater systems contain nutrients and minerals that are important to fertilizing land in the rainforest. It's no wonder the indigenous people of the jungle have traditionally had plenty of fish and melons to eat. Rainforest inhabitants are blessed, they do not generally starve in the jungle— nature provides.

On the opposite page is a heartbreaking photo of the results of an oil spill into the Amazon. Three once blue-orange-colored Amazon Kingfishers, flailing near a once magnificent green five-foot-diameter Amazon water lily, and two local indigenous people trying to save the birds are now all covered in the black oil of death. The life-giving waters of the Amazon are being polluted, this caption reads, because there are oil spills that threaten the water source for indigenous people as well as for the flora and fauna that need clean water.

A vivid memory opens up. I can hear Jack Kornfield saying in one of his teaching *dharma* talks in Marin, "As the Zen Buddhists say, 'What we need in the world today is to hear within us the sounds of the Earth crying.'"

Yes, it's raining tears—and the tears being shed are mine.

5
Black Amazon

"There are true lakes of oil, river banks abandoned to crude oil, clots of oil dot the water, black roots and sediments, toxic hydrocarbon emissions, and surface water iridescent with oil," Ronaldo states, standing over the local Iquitos newspaper, *La Región*.

"Just look at this," Ronaldo says, slapping the back of his hand on the lead article. "The recent leak of 3,000 barrels of oil in Peru's Amazon jungle will cause incalculable damage, according to scientists." He reads on aloud, "This recent oil spill is not a new problem. Two spills from the pipeline were reported in 2014 alone, when the equivalent of over 10,000 barrels of oil is said to have leaked from the pipeline." The shocking lead article title read, "Repeat Oil Spills Turning the Peruvian Amazon into a 'Sacrifice Zone' for Big Oil."

Ronaldo, a local Iquitos businessman friend of mine, cares deeply about the Amazon and its people. We are having a croissant together at a small sidewalk bistro Delirium Tremens—on the Malecón, the river's esplanade. Here the local Loretanos drink coffee by the gallon and swap true-or-not stories like there's no tomorrow. When the day is still cool, this is always a favorite meet-up bistro in Iquitos. Since a lot of tourists and hip locals hang out at this popular riverfront café, there's plenty of local newspapers, trendy magazines, and propaganda leaflets strewn on the tabletops.

Ronaldo leafs through a few more local newspapers, messing them up in his hurry. Everyone is fussing about the oil spill. Once oil was a welcomed source of revenues and opportunities for this area of the Amazon, now it is the source of loss, despair and destruction. Fueled by a refill of caffeine-rich coffee, Ronaldo finds yet another newspaper quote upon which to orate, "Since 2011 there have been at least 26 emergencies due to faults in oil pipelines. This disaster is the latest example of a string of accidents that have black-stained the Amazon, and a release of more than 2,300 barrels of oil in one year." He quickly adds his own aside, "These spills occur regularly and the impact will not easily disappear. Indigenous communities in the region also fish and hunt for food many of the animals now contaminated with oil."

Ronaldo takes a seat. In an exasperated huff he adds, "In Loreto where we live, Peru's northernmost and largest region, there are 500 territories and five indigenous reserves for people in voluntary isolation who have rejected any outside contact. My prediction is that now very likely these people have no fish or animals to eat, and no fresh water to drink." Ronaldo is on a roll, I have yet to get a word in edgewise.

The cool breeze coming off the river does nothing to quench Ronaldo's outrage. "Contamination and its negative impacts have been reported for decades by indigenous people, by government, by the news. Yet complaints and calls for action—cleanup, improved infrastructure, ecological impact studies—have gone unheard," he raves. "I've been saying this for years. From the 1970s onwards, the truth is that toxic production waters have been dumped into many Amazon River tributaries, and the facts are that oil pipelines are decades-old, corroded, rusty, and leaky."

We turn our attention to the overhead television, as the barista increases the volume for the local news report. "As many as 8,500 people living in the Amazonas region are believed to be affected by the most recent oil spill disaster," states a morning news reporter. "The oil company stated that contingency measures were immediately put into place following the spills and that rivers in the area were unaffected. However, local communities have reported that the spilt oil had begun to flow into the Amazon tributaries, as perimeter walls had overflowed due to heavy rains."

The television local news now shifts to an onsite in-the-jungle reporter, and the rant goes on. "Peru's national government declared a public health emergency on February 17 and met with community leaders three days later. But help was late to arrive, and by then, local men, women and children had come to the shores of the river to help with the cleanup."

The jungle reporter, with a few indigenous children at his side for full viewer impact, continues, "A number of children said they were paid two *soles,* less than one U.S. dollar, for every bucket of oil cleaned up." Turning the microphone over to a five-year-old village boy who comments in his still-girlish-voice, "We were gathering the oil with our hands and the oil fell on us. We asked for more money, but the engineer said no."

The reporter summed up by saying, "The children and those helping them were not warned about the dangers of continuous contact with oil, nor were they given special protection or training."

Standing behind the village boy is his father, stern-faced and obviously angry. He's chomping at the bit to have his say, too. The news reporter aims the microphone up to him, to capture the "indigenous voice" for viewers at home. "The production of oil is poisoning our indigenous communities of the Peruvian Amazon. During the last four decades the Peruvian government has allowed oil companies to drill on our ancestral lands without permission from our community." His voice is rising in the tension of this situation, just one more catastrophe in a long litany of disasters for these indigenous peoples. "Thousands of barrels of oil and toxic brine have contaminated the natural environment of the our jungle community, which has poisoned the rivers and caused serious health problems to our villagers."

"I ate food from my field after the spill," said Marina, an indigenous woman with two young children holding onto her hands. "Nobody told us it was dangerous, and I had nothing else to feed my children."

"Our major protein source is fish from the river, but now they are contaminated. Production for the sale and consumption of cassava, plantain, peanuts, cacao, and other food has suffered—they are totally covered in oil," said Manuel, a *ribereño* (riverside dweller) farmer states. Rubbing his ribcage with his left hand, he adds, "It is a serious food crisis."

The reporter then turns his face to the camera and concludes, "These indigenous communities who live in the depths of the Amazon, feel that they are invisible to this government and the rest of the planet. However, these deep jungle indigenous inhabitants have the same rights as the rest of the world. They have the right to lead a dignified and healthy life in their territory."

As the newscast begins to fade, a public service announcement runs along the bottom of the television screen in ticker-tape style that reads,

"The production of oil is poisoning the indigenous communities of the Peruvian Amazon. Act now and join their struggle to defend their rights to the land."

Media hype or not, where there's smoke there's fire. Everyone talks about the serious problems with big oil business these days. Oil controversy is on the television and radio, and in the news constantly. It's difficult to tell whether any news report is factual or biased in any way. Certainly this newscast did not give equal airtime to the oil companies themselves to respond publicly. Hope springs eternal that the oil companies will soon be able to defend their actions with a positive outcome for all.

The televised news report is over, and there's a noticeable increase in conversation buzz. Many at the café this morning are feeling the need to express themselves on the topic of the recent oil spill. Ronaldo introduces me to a friend of his, Cliver, an expert naturalist guide.

"Of equal concern is the effect of these oil spills on the Pacaya-Samiria Reserve," begins

Cliver in his professional guide voice. Now he has a bigger audience of café patrons listening in. "The Pacaya-Samiria is the second largest of Peru's 170 protected natural areas. It's located near the Amazon headwaters in Peru, where I give guided tours, and this reserve is home to some of the biggest wildlife populations in the Amazon," he states.

"We here in Peru are proud to say that the Pacaya-Samiria Reserve has been declared a Wetland of International Importance. It protects various species of flora and fauna at risk of extinction, like manatees, giant otters, and wild cacao trees. Pacaya-Samiria hosts 1000 plant species, 500 bird species, 100 mammal species, 140 reptile and amphibian species, and more than 250 fish species," Cliver quickly rattles off his naturalist-guide details.

A few more interested café patrons have leaned toward the table to join in listening to Cliver's pointed talk. "The Pacaya-Samiria is a flooded forest of major importance in fish reproduction. In the flooded season, I observe this bountiful cycle annually. The fish go into Pacaya-Samiria where all the forest floor debris—fallen fruits, insects, leaves from trees— serve as food supply," he continues. "Basically, Pacaya-Samiria becomes a 20,000-square-kilo- meter inland flooded forest, the largest in west- ern Amazonia, full of fish for our food. Then when the water goes down, the fish leave and go into the Amazon River and its tributaries where the fisherman catch them to feed their families. It is a beautiful thing to see, this rhythm of the life-giving Amazon River."

I am out of my element in this conversation, and in awe of his naturalist knowledge.

Cliver concludes with the clarity and convic- tion of a 20-year veteran as a naturalist guide, "The Pacaya-Samiria is by far the largest fish reproduction area in western Amazonia. This important Reserve, and the people who feed on its bounty, cannot withstand any more oil spills."

I don't want these bad situations to be happening in my heavenly Amazon. When I visit the Amazon, I wish all my experiences to be in the Garden of Eden that it is. I'm loathe to worry about such other matters while I'm here. The truth of all this does not set me free. I shake my head in the seriousness of it all, and reach for my cup of black coffee. "It's a black day for the world when the Amazon River turns black," I say, reading the future in the few coffee grounds floating in my *café negro.*

6
Temblor

Scientists say there may be a link between global warming, volcanoes, and tectonic plates beneath the surface that cause earthquakes. Climate change may play a critical role in activating certain faults in certain places. These stress and strain variations are capable of triggering a quake if that fault is ready to go. Scientists say that seismic faults are very sensitive to the small pressure changes brought by changes in the climate. What does this mean for all of us?

It's the holiday season and I'm back in my beloved Amazon once again. What a holiday treat, I couldn't be happier. I've always felt happy and safe in the jungle. As our *rápido* boat speeds its way to the lodge, I count my blessings. With each tree we pass, I give a silent prayer of gratitude for life itself.

The boat engine drones on, lulling me into a meditative state. What floats into the forefront of my mind at the moment, is the recent statement by Pope Francis about the holiday season upon us. A few weeks ago after terrorist attacks in Paris, he stated, "We are close to Christmas. There will be lights, there will be parties, bright trees, even Nativity scenes—all decked out— while the world continues to wage war. It's all a charade. The world has not understood the way of peace."

Pope Francis went on to say, "A war can be justified, so to speak, with many, many reasons, but with all the world as it is today, at war, piece-meal though that war may be—a little here, alittle there—there is no justification."

As his words echo in my mind, each word marked by a tree I see along the river's edge. The image of Pope's message is blurring into the message from the living souls of each of these trees. The trees before me begin to speak to me, "The world wages a war of destruction upon Mother Earth each time a tree in the Amazon is felled to the greed of commercialism. Yes, they say there are many reasons justifying the destruction of stands of Amazon trees over a century old. But, the world has not understood the way of peace with Nature."

The *rápido* hits a log in the river, jolting me out of my reverie. This rainy season approaching marks the end of the low-water season. The Amazon River is now free to gush life-giving waters everywhere, and with the newly rising waters comes the green plant flotsam and jetsam littering the waterways.

Once at the lodge, and after a simple lunch, it's now *siesta* time, the hottest part of the day. There's nothing quite like being rocked to sleep in the arms of loving Mother Nature. I feel the wooden floorboards beneath me bounce a bit, someone must be heading to my door. I may not get this nap after all. No one comes. The floorboards continue to shake. It must be Simba, the lodge's rescued adolescent pet ocelot prowling in the rafters. Nope, not her either. By now the shaking includes the entire room itself, and its contents. It's an earthquake, I quickly realize, having experienced them at home in the San Francisco Bay Area.

The earthquake continues steadily for another ten seconds or so. I'm not being rocked to sleep by Mother Nature, I'm being rocked awake, to alert.

I've never heard of nor experienced an earthquake in the Iquitos area or the jungle surrounds. Nothing damaged, the lodge and its occupants quietly settle back down to the day's *siesta*.

Late afternoon, the lodge guests and I all stumble out of our rooms and gather in the *comedor,* the dining room, for a cup of tea. "Did you feel that?" is nervously on everyone's lips. Into the *comedor* walks a neighboring shamana, who is stopping by to borrow some salt for a remedy she is making. I ask the elder shamana, nearing seventy I'd guess, if she had felt the earthquake.

"Yes", she replied nervously, "my very first earthquake experience ever."

Keying in on the astonished look in her eyes as big as saucers, I question further, "What do you think the earthquake means?"

"The *temblor,* earthquake, is Mother Nature's way of expressing her *pena* (pain) at the way we are treating her. It is her trembling sobbing at the disappointment she has in her children's—humankind's—lack of respect," she says. Then, as the shamana turns with a swish of her skirts and a point of her finger, she proclaims, "Humankind has become disenchanted with Mother Nature, and she with us—beware."

There was silence in the room. The wise old shamana walks out the door.

I let my *manzanilla,* chamomile, tea cool a bit longer in the hot afternoon air. Sitting quietly and silently, I ponder the many nuances of the Spanish word *pena*—pity, shame, sad, sorrow, problems. Mother Nature, indeed, must be truly feeling all of this, and more. It is perfectly natural that as she sobs, her shoulders heave and tremble—in this *temblor*—with her heart pain.

I feel the pain with her.

7
Jungle Fever

A *fever*—what happens when there is an infection or major dis-balance in the body. The purpose of a fever is to stimulate the immune system and to kill microbes by making it too hot for the invading microbes to survive. Fevers benefit humans by creating an inhospitable environment for invading organisms. What is *jungle fever?*

It's hot, *really* Amazon hot. At 9pm it is still so hot that I'm lying on my bed, naked, with a personal fan strung up from the rafters to bring some kind of cooling breeze. I'm waiting for the Amazon night to cool down its jungle fever.

I recall a few years back, meeting up in the Amazon with a self-made primatologist named Suzie. She had been bitten by the "jungle bug", as we call it, when she visited the Dallas Zoo twenty-five years earlier. Then and there she decided to dedicate her life to monkeys. She works in the Peruvian Amazon jungle on a funded monkey population project. According to Suzie's extensive jungle experience and Amazon-helpful-hints philosophy, it's always best to look at the netting gauge before picking your bed, because the larger the size of the holes in the netting the cooler you will be. True or not, you'll believe anyone who says it'll be cooler in the jungle if you follow this-or-that old wives' tale. I should have listened to Suzie before picking my bed this trip. The sweat is still dripping off my nude body. My sheets are getting soaked. It's hot.

Maybe the Amazon has a fever, my mind hallucinates in the heat of the night. What a concept, I muse. What if there is something to this. In the cool of the morning, I still can't shake the thought—*what if the Amazon herself has a fever?*

In the morning at breakfast, I notice that one of the lodge guests has inadvertently left their "Facts About the Amazon" book on the dining room table. Opening to the turned-down page in the book, I read that deforestation is a primary threat in the Amazon itself and is also a major contributor to global warming worldwide. By the year 2030 more than half of the forests in the Amazon could be gone. This loss would result in the release of billions of tons of carbon into the Earth's atmosphere.

The book goes on to explain that as the Amazon continues to lose soil and plant carbon, larger amounts of carbon dioxide and methane gases are released into the atmosphere— and that this pollution contributes to global warming.

Underlined in ink by the book's owner is the statement that the shrinking rainforest could result in the Amazon shifting from a carbon bank that keeps the element out of the atmosphere, to a source of carbon going into the atmosphere by the year 2050. More carbon dioxide in the air produces more greenhouse gas effects—more global warming. I wipe the sweat off my brow.

Over our early morning coffee, mesmerized by the Day-Glo hot pink-orange sunrise, all the lodge guests are commenting on the heat. The eco-group at the corner table invites me to join in on their conversation. I dare to posit my last night's hypothesis about the Amazon itself having a fever. One thirty-something San Francisco ecologist echoed the idea with his own embellishment—What if Gaia, our living Earth, has decided that the fever she has is a *global-warming-fever*.

All of us at the table, fueled by an early morning caffeine high, began to riff off his comment. Gaia knows that this fever is part of a healing process. The healing benefits of the fever might include ridding herself of unwanted organisms, we humans, by making it too hot for humans to live. The back-and-forth ping-pong banter quickened. Less humans means less forest destruction and less global warming. Thus, the global warming fever acts as a biofeedback loop to protect itself.

As the lodge jungle drum summons us to breakfast, we conclude that if deforestation were to stop, if humans got out of the way either physically or consciously, the natural forests in the Amazon would actually remove more carbon dioxide from the atmosphere than they emit, therefore reducing global warming.

My jungle heat-induced hallucination—global-warming-fever—may not so far-fetched after all.

8
Disappearing Medicines

A shaman's healing practices are a blend of medicine and spirit. The rainforest shamans are experts on the healing properties of the jungle's rich plant medicines. These shamans have an intimate relationship with the healing spirits of nature and of the plants, which they summon on behalf of the patient during the healing.

In addition to the healing power of nature itself, shamans rely on the potent pharmacology of the plants themselves to help heal the physical causes of maladies and diseases. Deforestation also wipes out powerful plant medicines, along with the trees. Deforestation prevents any opportunity to discover new plant cures for to-day's intractable diseases, such as AIDS and cancer. Many plant species that potentially hold the key to new life-saving medicines are facing destruction daily. Will the ancient ways of Amazonian shamanism and the powerful plant medicines they use fall into extinction?

One sultry evening in Iquitos, just after 7pm when the day had cooled only a bit after sunset, I head to a meeting at UCP (Universidad Científica del Perú), a private university in Iquitos. In the *motokar* along Av. Abelardo Quiñones, the dust that kicks up from the *motokar* ahead sticks to the sweat on my arms and face. I am meeting with six of the university's scientists, botanists and biologists, all members of UCP's Amazon Research Field Station. The meeting is to take place at 7:30pm in one of UCP's empty classrooms.

It's now 7:30pm, and I'm the only one in the room. I want to be on time in case anyone actually shows up on time. Normal "time" is something I have come to call "jungle time" here in Iquitos, as everyone usually shows up later than scheduled. By 7:55pm, we are all present and accounted for. The purpose of the meeting is for me to learn about all the good work being done at their Research Field Station deep in the jungle, and for the team to meet me to see what I can do for them financially or with networking connections.

Since they know I am a pharmacist, they gear their presentation around plant medicines and pharmaceuticals. One young botanist begins the presentation laying the groundwork for discussion. He states that the World Health Organization reports that approximately 75-80% of the world's population uses plant medicines either in part or entirely as curatives. Generally, this is out of necessity, since many cannot afford the high cost of pharmaceutical drugs, nor are they readily available.

I enter the discussion with a commonly known fact that even today in Western Medicine, some 25% of modern prescription drugs contain at least one compound derived or patterned after compounds derived from plants. I punctuate my statement by adding that I believe that what medicinal chemists are desperately seeking, Mother Nature often already has in stock. "Mother Nature is still the cheapest and the best chemist," I add.

A fifty-something professor of ethnobotany stands up to take the floor. His full shock of black hair is pressing against his shirt collar. I notice because I'm always amazed how I've yet to meet a Peruvian with any kind of bald spot. He adds his own words of wisdom, "Tropical rainforests, such as we have in the Amazon, are called the 'world's largest pharmacy'. Indigenous peoples of the Amazon rainforest have used various plants since antiquity as remedies and cures for their health and survival. Scientists are now discovering that many of these botanicals are potentially valuable sources for new drugs to treat cancer, AIDS, arthritis, diabetes, and Alzheimer's disease. Anticancer drugs, quinine for malaria, curare as a muscle relaxant, are only a few of the helpful drugs have already been discovered from Amazon botanicals. We owe our relief from diseases and maladies to many of the Amazon medicinal plants that have become modern medicines."

"Not only are medicinal plants of the Amazon facing extinction," he goes on, "but so is the knowledge of where to find and how to use these medicinal plants. Such plant wisdom is kept alive by generations of shamans and traditional healers. With the disappearance of the Amazon indigenous cultures, and along with that the disappearance of village shamans, comes the disappearance of the traditions and knowledge of medicinally useful plants from the Amazon. We still have a chance to document them. At UCP's Research Field Station, one of our focuses is to investigate the various medicinal plants used by local villages near the Field Station, and what conditions they treat using those plants."

He concludes his detailed comments with a powerful statement, "Time is running out. Our forests and plant lore are dying out. Every time a forest in the Amazon is felled, it is as if a corner pharmacy has closed its doors. Every time a native healer or shaman dies, the keepers of the plant lore, a virtual library of knowledge dies with them."

I look at a statement in the Research Field Station's brochure: The people of the jungle, usually the shamans, are the keepers of the medicinal plant lore. Plants are their medicine. Shamans are medicinal plant experts, as well as the village doctors. Without the plant knowledge handed down through the generations of these shamans, the indigenous people of the deep jungles—and many of us in the modern world—would not be as healthy today.

I recall an enlightening experience many years ago. Walking along a medicinal plant trail deep in the forest, my *maestro* was teaching me about the uses of medicinal plants. One by one, he told me about the benefits of this tree or that plant. It struck me wide-eyed as he informed me that diabetics would benefit from taking medicinal doses of a couple of different plants and trees.

I stopped him dead on the trail. "How can you tell if someone has diabetes?" I inquired with a slightly joking tone in my voice. After all, he doesn't have a glucose meter or a diabetes kit of any kind to diagnose and treat diabetes.

Expecting to trick him, I was astonished by the wisdom in his jungle-logic reply, "You can tell if someone has diabetes because when they urinate in the jungle, the ants run quickly towards the sweet urine. And I can tell if my remedies are working when the ants do not congregate around the patient's fresh urine anymore. There is no more sugar in their urine." A simple and profound answer.

Shamans are the most endangered species of the Amazon. In most of the communities in the Amazon area in which I work the local shamans have died, taking with them their precious plant medicine knowledge. My *maestro* is aging, as are many of the others. At almost 80 years old, he is one of the last of the old forest-born-and-trained shamans in the area.

I have been fortunate to apprentice with one of the last of the old Amazon jungle shamans. Born deep in the jungles of Peru, his entire education from boyhood consisted of the teachings of his mother and grandmother, both shamans, so generations of knowledge were passed onto him. His classroom—the jungle itself.

The old ways of shamanism in the Amazon are dying out. Few of the youth of the Amazon want to apprentice anymore. Even the indigenous villagers, when asked, would rather take a pill or have a shot for what ails them. There are fewer and fewer village shamans living. The knowledge of the use of plant medicines within the indigenous villagers themselves is often scant to nil. It is clearly a challenge for today's village healers to obtain plant knowledge if all the old shamans in their area have died, and along with them so does their medicinal plant knowledge.

I am with a group of Iquitos student ethno-botanists and their teacher, Juan. They have come to the lodge on a project to identify and label the medicinal plants and trees that surround the lodge. After they finish their day in the field and shower, they head to the lodge bar. Over a couple pisco sours, their teacher is in the mood to share an amusing, but telling, story.

The story goes that a fellow colleague ethno-botanist friend of Juan's was hired by Shaman Pharmaceuticals, then of South San Francisco, California, to be part of a team whose focus was to obtain medicinal plants in the greater Iquitos Amazon region that might possibly become pharmaceuticals.

First, a highly-skilled team was organized to develop an interview sheet that they would use with various shamans from different villages to obtain consistent information about a certain purported medicinal plant. The indigenous uses of plants by native healers and shamans can offer strong clues to the biological activities for these plants. Ultimately, research and testing would be used to verify the authenticity of this information.

The team included of members of the ethnobotanical, medical, anthropological, and ethnopharmaceutical fields of expertise. Their job was to create an interview sheet as thorough and objective as possible so that there would be no room for subjective or hearsay information. From this interview sheet, these scientists would obtain information from the local jungle shamans about which plants are used for what purpose, the names of these plants, where the plants are located, which plant part is used as medicine, how to prepare the plant medicine, and dosages. Later, there would be research to verify the authenticity of the information. The process of creating this serious interview sheet took many months, at an expense of almost one million dollars, according to Juan.

Armed with their ideal scientific interview sheet, the next step was to find local shamans who were willing to be interviewed and to share their plant knowledge. This was a most difficult step. After all, the ethnobotanical teacher told us, why should any shaman give out their preciously-earned generations of proprietary plant medicine information.

The story goes that after several weeks of going from village to village to find a shaman who was willing to work with them, they had their first breakthrough when a female shaman from the Napo River area agreed to be interviewed. After an hour of interviews, the final question on the interview sheet remained— where did the woman obtain her information. Did the local jungle shamans learn their plant medicine information from their *maestro* shaman, or another shaman in a neighboring village, and so forth.

This last important question was asked of the woman shaman. She began her answer by naming a few other local village shamans as sources for her information. Juan says that she then excitedly jumped up from her chair and hurried to the back area of her *tambo* hut. Moments later, as the story goes, she returned and proudly handed them an additional source of her information—a copy of Jeanne Rose's *Herbal,* a textbook written by an American herbalist from San Francisco, California.

The last laugh was on the scientific team, according to Juan, because they assumed they were researching in remote, untainted areas of the jungle. Juan's story illustrates that the days of finding pristine forests with indigenous healers who still hold the authentic uninfluenced medicinal plant lore are indeed becoming fewer and farther between.

The authentic indigenous shamans raised and taught in the jungles of the Amazon who remain living are mostly 70 years old or more. Alas, with them goes a wealth of knowledge of medicinal species of plants and organisms.

We must preserve indigenous plant wisdom by preserving indigenous healing wisdom and the shamans who carry this knowledge. And we must do all we can to preserve the rainforests of the Amazon, the pharmacies of the forest. Today, more than one-fifth of the Amazon rainforest has already been destroyed and is gone forever. The Amazon rainforests and their shamans are irreplaceable. I believe it is a call to action for all of us.

I am saddened at the disappearance of our pharmacies in the rainforest and the fading-away of the shamans, keepers of the plant wisdom. My heart aches at the thought of what could be done, should be done, is being done—and what *isn't* being done.

9
A Living National Treasure

I look down at my *maestro's* aging hands—the hands that have taught me, disciplined me, and loved me for nearly twenty-five years. They are chestnut brown and gnarled, like the knots of his forest flora friends the medicinal plant trees. His fingernails are stained orange-brown from the sap and juices of thousands of medicinal plants and trees that have over a lifetime given up their powerful medicines to this old shaman so that he may heal others. The dirt of a thousand plant gardens is permanently embedded under his nails. If only these hands could talk—*yes, they can talk!*

Today, we are walking along a new medicinal plant trail and garden my *maestro* is creating. I watch his earth-colored wrinkled leathery hands do their magic—planting, identifying, labeling medicinal plants and vines and trees. His hands do talk, in a way, by creating yet another living library and rainforest pharmacy of nature's healing botanicals along this new medicinal plant trail.

As we move along the jungle path, the forest plants and trees and flowers come alive for my maestro. "This is the *pichirina* tree. The orange sap from its leaves is good for sores, wounds, and skin fungus," he says with the knowing conviction of much experience. His eyes light up as he reaches toward a curious-looking vine. "This is *uña de gato* (cat's claw)," he states, while pointing to the curved claw-looking spines under each leaves. "I call it the heal-all vine. It's good for a wide variety of ailments," he says with delight as he continues to give me a list of a dozen different uses for the bark of the cat's claw vine.

I happen to know some pharmacology of this cat's claw vine, and indeed, there is beginning research suggesting potential anti-inflammatory, anticancer, and immuno-stimulant properties. While more research is needed, the difficulty in getting that done in the U.S.A. is that one cannot "patent a plant", so there is no money as incentive to do more research. Thus, we do not know the active ingredients or the mechanisms of actions of these powerful medicinal plants, that could potentially save lives from difficult to treat and intractable conditions.

As he walks and talks and teaches me, my *maestro* becomes one with the forest and its wonder around him. As I get near him to look at the leaf of a particular plant in his hand, I get a whiff of the natural sweet smell emanating from him. I call it his "jungle aftershave". After all these years in the jungle he has taken on the enchanting aroma of the perfumed wood of the jungle, with the hint of the soil and plants that are his medicine—he is the jungle personified.

As if in his own version of Alice in Wonderland, he slips into another dimension. His visage is increasingly difficult to distinguish from the trees around him, as he becomes the living voice for these powerful medicines. As he continues to introduce me to the various trees and plants by name and characteristics and uses, the forest becomes alive for me, too. The spirit of each tree and plant steps forward to greet me upon introduction.

We round the bend of the medicinal plant trail head-on into an enormous buttressed tree. My *maestro* steps over many snake-like surface roots as he approaches this majestic 100-foot-tall tree. "This is *ojé*, a medicinal fig tree. The white resin is used to treat intestinal parasites. You mix the latex with orange juice or sugarcane juice, to open the mouth of the parasite with a sweet taste, as you poison the parasite with the latex," he instructs. "The locals call it *Doctor Ojé* because they swear by its power. But it's toxic, you have to know the right amount, and how and when to give it," he cautions, shaking a finger.

"That's the problem with the knowledge of the uses of medicinal plants these days. Even if the locals know which plant to use for which condition, they do not know the correct dosage or their side-effects," my *maestro* adds, looking down and shaking his head.

I'm reminded of a recent conversation with a gentleman in Iquitos who knows many shamans in the Iquitos area. He said to me, "The current younger shamans, also dwindling in number, largely do not know how to use the medicinal plants. They only want to 'give blessings', not 'doctor' people. Most of them have not been raised in the jungle with the plant medicines all around them, nor have they had the opportunity to learn plant medicines from the old shamans— the old shamans are all dying out. *Qué lástima,* what a pity."

Yes, there is a smattering of Amazonian medicinal plant information available in a few books or online. Generally, they give the Spanish name, English name, scientific name, and a list of local uses. But often they do not give information about which part of the plant is used, how it is prepared, side effects, dosage, nor length of treatment. And certainly these few books are not available in jungle villages as references to those who can read. All of this detailed knowledge is dying along with the old shamans.

It feels good and right to be able to support and honor my *maestro*—my deepest thanks to shaman don Antonio Montero Pisco—in what may be a capstone project for him at this late time in life, his culminating medicinal plant project. He is in his power when he is teaching about medicinal plants, doctoring the villagers, and passing on his knowledge. My dream is that his complete knowledge of medicinal plants be archived before it's too late. He is truly a national treasure—yes, a *living national treasure,* to be sure.

10
You've Been Gone Too Long

We all long to go home—to what's familiar, to our resting place, to ourselves. One time, back home in California during a healing session for me, two decades ago at a time when my life was in complete turmoil, I remember listing my overall presenting symptoms in one phrase— "all I want is to go home". I didn't even consciously know what I meant by that statement at the time. Now, I can say that I am at home with myself, thanks to the medicine of the jungle and its healing.

Now, many moons later, I am returning to my beloved Amazon jungles, my second visit to Peru for the year. I am so glad to be back in the jungle once again. My body is hurting, aching all over, as a body this age is prone to do after just having finished writing a book manuscript. I am in dire need of relief.

Our *rápido,* speedboat, is full-throttle ahead, as if to outrun the oppressing equatorial jungle heat of high noon. As we full-speed-ahead on the wide Amazon River, we near a series of familiar tributaries, a route I know well after decades of travel through these waters. In the moment, I am startled to sense that we are in unfamiliar territory. Perhaps I am just de-hydrated and a bit delusional, I think to myself.

"Where are we?" I ask my guide, "I don't seem to know where we are."

Jorge explains, "The river is so low that we have to take this route around the other side of this landmass to get to the lodge. The normal route is impassible at this time." I hope we get there soon, I say under my breath.

We round the river's curve and there is the lodge, at last. While the staff scurries to unload my luggage from the boat, I head directly to the *comedor* (dining room) for a tall glass of cold *cocona* juice. The thick orange-yellow juice rehydrates me and gives me some much-needed natural sugar to refresh my body.

Exhausted from the heat and the ride, I head pronto to my room for a shower and a rest before lunch. Home at last, I drift into reverie to the waning chatty late-morning bird conversations and the thick slap sounds of river water swatting the muddy shores.

Somewhere between here and there, my consciousness melds into oneness with the sense-surround-sounds of nature filling my head. I begin to shift my focus into my dream-time internal experience.

In dreamtime, I'm back in San Francisco, California. *Jungle Medicine,* my first book, is finally finished. Both wrists ache from too much computer time and I'm exhausted from having run the gauntlet of writing a book. I am so looking forward to this much needed, and greatly earned, getaway in the Amazon. The deep relaxation of the Amazon's bosom is calling me. Flying out of SFO and leaving the U.S., the western world begins to disappear. Then taking off from Jorge Chávez International Airport out of Lima, Peru, the busy city lights below fade into the sky. In the last leg of leaving my modern life behind, the jungle border town of Iquitos merges and fades into the tall trees on the Amazon River's edge as our river boat winds its way deeply into the jungle, *la selva,* my refuge.

In my reverie, my *maestro's* visage comes slowly into focus, he awaits me at the dock of the lodge. Together we stroll into the dining room area of the lodge, where there are two tall glasses of cold watermelon juice. We chatter like magpies, each eager to get the update on our lives since last we met. The long shadows of late afternoon creep across our chairs, as time has disappeared in our rapt conversation.

"Tell me, how's your health?" my *maestro* finally asks.

"My wrists really hurt," I answer bluntly with a lot of painful energy behind the words.

Dreamtime is not linear. Next I sense that it is late afternoon and, as usual at day's end, my maestro gives me a *limpieza,* fragrant cleansing herbal bath, and a tobacco healing.

What seems like many dreamtime hours and many healings and days later, my *maestro* asks me, "Well, now how do your wrists feel?"

"They feel fine now," I say, watching his head nod in agreement. I added, almost as an afterthought, "I always feel fine in the jungle."

He takes both my hands into his. Looking me straight in the eye, he lovingly responds, "That is the teaching, my dear. Your problem is not actually the pain that you're complaining about. The pain is simply Spirit's way of telling you that you've been gone too long—too long away from the healing and life-giving energies of deep Nature."

"It is true for all of us when we hurt," are his last fading words as he disappears into the back-drop of dreamtime.

I sank into a profound sleep that refreshed and relaxed me. All I needed to do was "be here" and let the life-giving sights, sounds and smells of the Amazon heal me and bring me home.

Thank you, Spirit.

11
Disconnection—
A Disease with a Cure

As a new and naïve graduate from the College of Pharmacy, I truly believed that pharmaceuticals would stamp out disease one pill at a time. Somewhere in my young mind, I thought that disease happened to us, that we had no responsibility for causing it or curing it, and that the great cure of our generation was the invention of modern medicine and pharmaceuticals. What I have come to learn from my apprenticeship in Amazonian shamanism, as well as from my own medical conditions—for my cancer, I needed the surgeon and the shaman—is that modern medicine and pharmaceuticals are tools, not answers, to good health.

Sitting in my Iquitos second floor *apartamento* overlooking the Amazon River, I'm alone on this completely gray-washed rainy day. It rains some 260 days a year in this equatorial rainforest. Well-rested, my mind is clear and open. In this mindspace, I wonder what the modern medical definition of disease is. One googled definition that just popped up on my computer screen says that the medical definition of disease is: an impairment of the normal state of the living animal or plant body or one of its parts that interrupts or modifies the performance of the vital functions, is typically manifested by distinguishing signs and symptoms, and is a response to environmental factors (as malnutrition, industrial hazards, or climate), to specific infective agents (as worms, bacteria, or viruses), to inherent defects of the organism (as genetic anomalies), or to combinations of these factors.

I wait for the kettle of water and tea to boil, steeping along with it is the wordy definition of disease I'd just read. Each rigorous word is churning and tumbling like tea leaf bits in the boiling pot of my mind. The words impairment, interruption, modification, are roiling around in my thoughts.

As I wait for the tea to steep, my mind easily slips into the reverie of remembrance in the fogginess of the day's climate. My thoughts and visions shift to a day some twenty years ago at my *maestro's tambo,* my teacher's forest shelter.

"In your experience, what is the cause of disease?" I inquire.

"In the world of the shaman, the one primary cause of dis-ease and disease is *disconnection,"* he answers back easily and assuredly.

I am quiet for a moment, taking in his reply with consideration.

I am suddenly pulled back into the present moment, as the hot cup of tea almost burns my hand. Indeed true, I think to myself. Modern medicine defines disease as impairment, interruption, modification. And the shaman says disease is disconnection from health. Yes, it clicked. They're different words to explain the same principle.

Looking out over the hazy Amazon, sipping a cup of warming *anís* tea on this coolish day, my mind "made the connection" in the deepest sense.

Connectivity. We utterly rely on it in everyday life. Connectivity is an oft-used word that can, in everyday life, easily lose the power of its deepest meaning. I snap back from my reverie to reality and inspired by my muse, the Amazon, reach for my notebook. My mind is telling me to outline a short talk on the power of connectivity. I write. Without connectivity, everything grinds to a halt. Many of us have lost the full understanding of connectivity's importance, or in many cases have not developed such an understanding.

A simple example for my talk comes to mind. If there is a power disruption things that run on electricity will not work. In my native Minnesota when there is a heavy snowstorm the roads become quickly paralyzed and no one can get to their jobs or the grocery store. I remember being forced to drive a snowmobile to work in order to open the pharmacy in my hometown outside of Minneapolis on one blizzardy morning. We all understand that simple example—if the systems we live by go down or get disconnected, then our day-to-day lives are disrupted until the problems are fixed or reconnected. We all see and feel the connectivity of these everyday systems upon which we have come to rely.

On a more personal scale, stress plays a huge role in our health and effectiveness in life. The welcomed cool of the day, the pastel setting sun, and the rising volume of night sounds all heighten my energy. I continue writing. When we go into a stress reaction there is a tendency to "disconnect" as a protective mechanism. We are thankfully hard-wired to disconnect in these situations. The real problem occurs when we get stuck in the disconnect of fight-or-flight. The shamans call this fear, *susto*.

When I ask my *maestro* to help me understand the nature of *susto*, he replies, "*Susto* is an attack on the spirit of someone from a traumatic event. *Susto* happens to you when a tree falls on your jungle hut, or when your dugout capsizes in a tropical storm, or you see someone attacked with a *machete*. You receive a big shock and are afraid—that's easy to understand."

"But I see another kind of *susto*," he continues, "in the eyes and souls of the tourists who visit here. I have now come to understand that people of the modern world suffer *susto* due to the chipping away at their souls because of the many modern-life daily pressures and fears. When these dull-eyed, energy-depleted tourists ask me to give them an energy healing, they tell me that they work long hours at meaningless jobs, put their children through universities without a guarantee of a job for them, pay a high amount for healthcare, and taxes take a lot of their paycheck. Nothing as seemingly catastrophic as a one-time event such as the fallen tree or capsized dugout, perhaps, but rather the subtler fears—that are very real—that little by little eat away at the *energia positiva* of their spirit. The result is the same—*susto*. Over time, these many modern life fears have the same traumatic disconnect damage to your soul as a one-time momentary huge fear-inducing event."

As a result of this modern-life disconnection we go down the rabbit hole and experience the sequence of dis-attention, dis-connection, dis-communication, dis-regulation, dis-order, dis-ease, and even disease. All of the issues of dis-eases—and sometimes diseases—that come up as a result of this sequence are merely symptoms, not causes. As we all know, the most effective way to resolve an issue or condition is by addressing the cause, not the symptom. The cause is the disconnection, not the resulting issue or condition.

A while back, at a time when Marin, California was known as "the breast cancer capital of the world", I remember vividly listening to a radio conversation with a UCSF physician specializing in breast cancer. It was a wake-up call for me to hear this physician say, "When a woman comes to me with a breast cancer diagnosis, the first thing I treat is her fear." This fear, this *susto,* is the great disconnect. In this disconnect, we are unable to let in the life-giving energy of the life force.

We also have "ecological disconnect". I like that term. We can carry on with this manic, headlong, polluting and disconnected state of living until Mother Nature decides to pull the plug. Mother Nature may simply decide that the undesired effects of mankind are like having a bad case of head lice. She may simply decide to shake us all off her global head to rid herself of the discomfort of mankind.

A healthy environment provides us with breathable air, drinkable water and all our food. We need to be connected to the ecological interplay of all that is our environment—including ourselves. We can either work with the environment or against it. I believe that the absolute bottom line is that if the environment dies, it takes mankind with it.

It does not do any good merely to blame oil companies or governments, as we have been doing, for what ails us. What ails us stems from a disregard for Nature within ourselves. This disregard jeopardizes the human species. Make no mistake about it—Nature will survive. But it is not certain that we will. My *maestro* once made this stinging comment, "Connie, remember that if humans vanish from the face of the Earth tomorrow, there would not be an animal, bird, fish, or even a plant that would not give out a big sigh of relief."

The Disease of Disconnect is dangerous and powerful. I'm winding up my notes for the call-to-action of my new talk on connectivity. It's late in the evening, and swarms, I mean swarms, of bugs have all found the light bulb under which I am writing. I conclude my notes. The coming ecological disaster we all fear will happen is already here. This ecological disaster has happened—and is happening—because we continue to separate ourselves from the world around us. We theoretically understand not-separate-ness, but do we really internalize our inter-connected-ness in the depths of our being, and live life accordingly? This is our calling—to be even more committed to living lives of connection wherever and however we can. It starts with the daily choices we make and extends to being willing to challenge ourselves to grow in ecological consciousness beyond our limited lives, and to lead a life of powerful service.

I make a few notes in the margins as I wrap up my thinking for the evening. I conclude there

are two forms of abuse that we humans participate in—the exploitation of the natural
resources of the Earth, and the denial of Nature
Being within ourselves. We are interdepend-
ent—one and the same. We cannot love one, and
disregard the other. The Original Sin of mankind is in leaving the Garden of Eden, so to
speak. Now we humans have placed ourselves in
voluntary exile from Nature.

I close my notebook and grab a rosewood
rocking chair to take to the edge of the veranda
overlooking the river. As I take in the river's
cooling breezes of the night air, I realize there is
a second half of my talk yet to be written. The
Amazon River is always a source of inspiration
for my thoughts and writings. Looking out over
the vast 180-degree river view and taking it all
in, my eyes focus on an old wooden boat, grey-
brown with age and no paint, in the foreground.
With utmost stillness, a solitary man stands in
the center of his boat, watching closely the
black, still river waters around him. His boat
adrift with no motor running, with his sinewy

earth-brown arms glistening with sweat in the moonlight, he is poised for action with his heavy fishing net in hand.

I notice two pink dolphins surfacing nearby, so smooth, wet and sleek, looking for a late river fish dinner, too. Suddenly, at the precise moment of action, he circles his fishnet overhead in a grand flourish. The boat rapidly circles the school of fish, with the fisherman's body and whirling fishnet providing the momentum for the action. Snap. Plop. The net lands. Puff, pooph, puff. The pink dolphins surface for air, then plunge for the hunt, too. I am witnessing an orchestra of the actions and sounds all playing the same ancient symphony of the interconnectedness of life—the fisherman, the pink dolphins, and the school of fish. This has been performed for millennia in these ancient waters. This ecstatic moment of becoming one with the unfolding scene, I see—as one—the fisherman, his father, grandfather, great grandfather, great-great grandfather, and all the ancestral men of his lineage performing the same ancient fishing dance of life.

I recall the simplicity of the second half of my *maestro's* first statement about disconnection being the primary cause of disease/dis-ease. His solution is a powerful lesson for us all. If disconnection is the problem, connection is the answer. When I had reached the burn-out point in my life, my *maestro's* advice was clear and direct, "Spend time in deep Nature. It will heal your body, mind, and soul. It is the role of shamans to help connect people to the life force, however they can.

12
Ecological Medicine—
Connection as Cure

"Connection is the solution to many of our diseases and dis-eases," says my *maestro*. And he is quick to add, "Disconnection is our primary problem in life. It is our job as shamans to help people connect back up to the life-force, however we can." Ecological Medicine is the medicine of connection.

Can this diminutive dark-skinned man, born and raised in the jungle, calling himself a shaman—uneducated by our standards and un-exposed to the concepts of our modern world—

be telling a core truth? I decide to do some online research now that I'm back in Iquitos where there is an internet connection. Firing up my laptop, all the minute gnats in my *apartamento* swarm along with me to the desktop screen that is now lighting up the corner of the room.

I don't have to look far. The World Health Organization (WHO), whose primary role is to direct and coordinate international health, thinks similarly. The WHO, as stated in their 1948 preamble, defines health: Health is a state of complete physical, mental and social well-being and not merely the absence of disease or infirmity. The Definition has not been amended since 1948—they got it right the first time.

We know that a balanced mind and a healthy body affect our well-being. Even social well-being is a factor in health. Harmonious relationships we have within our community, friends, and family affect our health and well-being.

As a pharmacist and medical insider, I inherently lean toward the organic reasons for illness. My medical training tells me my thyroid cancer was eradicated over twenty years ago by the thyroidectomy surgical intervention. My shamanic training tells me there were additional spiritual factors involved. So, I let the doctors do their Western Medicine protocol while I lit candles to invoke any and all deeper healing necessary to make sure I got to the core of what was ailing me.

After my thyroidectomy, the protocol called for an additional radiation treatment using the radioactive iodine principle. No thyroid replacement medication was given to me for five weeks following surgery so my body could be bled of any residual thyroid in my system. Then, by giving a dose of radioactive iodine—residual thyroid tissue would absorb the iodine, and along with it the radiation—any remaining thyroid would get zapped.

With no thyroid replacement medication in my system for five weeks I gradually became weaker and weaker as my metabolism slowed to almost a halt. I was so weak I could not drive a car or balance my checkbook. This weakened state was perfect for "letting go" to my spiritual intention of getting to the deepest healing possible.

One rainy afternoon at my home in Marin, California, while staring at the candle that I kept perpetually lit, in my weakened state I began to hallucinate—seeing the spirits of my family around me. Surprised, I welcomed them and asked them why they came to visit. They told me that I had called them forth with my intention of deep healing from my cancer. They said that each family member had their personal life story to tell me and asked me to listen closely.

My father stepped forth and told me how his love for all of us kept him working long hours at his business to keep the family together, especially since my mother suffered from bouts of mental health issues and one of my sisters had an intellectual development disorder— when I was growing up, we called it mental retardation. Wow, what an insight at that moment. All my years growing up I had thought of my father as an absentee-dad, not much caring for the family life at home. How wrong I had been.

Then my mother came forward and told her story, followed by each of my sisters and their stories. Each of them gave me a profound insight as to my misperception of their "hurt to me" as a child, and how I still carried those wounds in my heart. Humbled by their stories, I thanked them and asked them what their purpose was in being here with me that day.

Their answer was profound and direct, "If you want to 'live' after this bout of cancer, you must give up your misperception of what happened or didn't happen to you as a child. You must now, in this moment, let go of the resentment and energy around the 'stories' you've been carrying about your family all these years."

I said, "I don't know how to do that, even after countless forgiveness seminars I've attended."

They responded firmly, "You must find a way, right now and forever."

With that, my entire body went into multiple energy spasms as I let go in a deep and profound way, because I wanted to Live—with a capital L—in every way possible. Powerful are the ways of Spirit to heal perceived and real family issues.

Health is multifactorial. My online research points out that our physical health is also dependent on the physical health of our environment. The World Health Organization also declares: Environmental Health includes all the physical, chemical, and biological factors external to a person, and all the related factors impacting behaviors. It encompasses the assessment and control of those environmental factors that can potentially affect health. It is targeted towards preventing disease and creating health-supportive environments. All this complex wording describes what every shaman knows as a fundamental truth of life.

As my head wraps itself around this wordy definition, my heart opens up and vividly recalls an experience that happened over twenty years ago—as if it were real in this moment.

Returning to the Amazon, alone for the first time, my job is to help my soon-to-be *maestro* create a medicinal plant garden. He appoints the job of weed whacking to me and hands me a 24-inch sharply honed *machete* to clear an area in the forest in which to plant. He also gives me a broom with which to sweep the dried fallen leaves off the cleared forest floor. Not speaking a word of Spanish, my jungle job becomes a working silent meditation—sweeping and sweeping in Zen-like meditation for hours and hours. Every day, day after day, I show up at the garden with *machete* in hand to do my job in silence. Every dusk, the magical in-between time of day, the shaman gives me an Amazonian blessing with *mapacho* (tobacco) smoke and *icaros*—the shaman's ancient healing incanta-tions, partly sung and partly whistled. Not really understanding the meaning of all these daily rituals, I decide to just relax and let the enchant-ment of these beautiful and other-worldly songs fill my ears, my heart and my soul.

Little do I know that my soon-to-be-*maestro* is already working his magic. One night in my *sueños,* dreams, after a few weeks of weed whacking and healings, all is revealed. This Amazonian shaman is not assigning me the gar-den weed whacking job randomly. He does it on purpose. He wants me to foster my own natural wildness and garden world within my heart. Not only is he having me weed whack a jungle clear-ing for the medicinal plant garden, but also on a spiritual level I am weed whacking the "jungle" in my heart—clearing away the twisted negative debris in my heart to make possible my own flourishing loving garden in my own heart.

Because of the mud and rain, I wear rubber boots every day to do my garden work. It was no surprise that after four days I notice that my right big toe had become infected. I look down at my red inflamed toe without worry—after all, I have a couple different antimicrobial creams and three different oral antibiotics in my well-packed pharmacist's first-aid kit. Just as I am about to do some self-treatment, it occurs to me to take this problem, minor as it is, to the shaman. I am curious to see what a jungle shaman will do to treat my toe.

Grabbing a guide as a translator, we head pronto to the shaman's hut. Looking down at my infected toe, he rubs his chin and informs me, "You have some kind of jungle-rot. And since there's not a medical doctor around for many miles, I am going to be your doctor. We want to treat this minor infection now, so that the infection does not become systemic." Little does he know that I have all kinds of antibiotic creams and pills to do the job, if all else fails. So I let him do his healing on me—let's see what happens.

He promptly gathers up six different kinds of plant leaves, a papaya, and some salt, out of which he makes a healing foot bath. Then he places this medicinal plant mixture directly in the sun to macerate, soak, for a bit. Such fresh green medicine. I assure myself that all this foot bath remedy-making seems a rational treatment approach to my Western Medicine thinking. Then, to my surprise, my *maestro* takes out his *machete* and begins to sharpen it against a stone, saying, "I think you're going to lose your toenail, so I'm preparing my *machete* as a first-aid tool if we need to pry off your toenail." My eyes spring open as big as saucers, and my heart begins to pound. Needless to say, I am rooting for the medicinal plant foot bath, rather than going under the *machete*-knife surgery.

The vibrant green aromatic medicinal plant foot bath is ready. The shaman takes my right foot into his left hand and begins pouring cala-bash scoopfuls of the warmish healing foot bath mixture over my foot. Ever so gently, he contin-ues to pour scoop after scoop over my right foot. With much care and concern he bends down closely to examine my right toe, then continues to pour more healing plant mixture over my foot. As the shaman does this with great attention, I can't help but think of the term "attending physician"—the physician in charge of total patient care. My heart, opening to his tender care, silently whispers to me, "If love heals, then my toe will surely be healed." In that moment I realize the healing power of caring attendance, and how often that is missing in our overworked Western Medicine healthcare.

By afternoon, a few local villagers gather around the "shaman and the *gringa*" healing event taking place. They are curious, asking, "What is happening here, what's the problem?" I motion for the guide-translator to tell them, "It's nothing at all, just a small toe infection." Soon, a few more villagers join the growing crowd, asking the same questions. And again, I give dismissive shoulder shrugs, not really understanding what all the fuss is about. A few more passersby stop to take a look, adding to the number of gawkers. Not understanding Spanish, the community gossip being passed around sounds like mumbling to me.

Then, like lightening, it suddenly dawns on me what this is all about—the healing power of community. In an indigenous society, if I were a farmer, I would not be able to go out into the fields to tend my crops with a bum foot. If I were an indigenous mother with five children, I wouldn't be able to fix their dinner or wash their clothes if I were laid up. Bottom line, all these villagers do indeed care about my infected toe, because it is important that one be healthy within community life to be able to perform family and community functions. If I had simply put a bandage with antibiotic cream on my toe— as I would do back home—and went about my day, I would have missed the opportunity for this positive healing energy of community with friends, family and colleagues concerned about my health and welfare.

By the end of the second day of herbal foot baths, my toe is not markedly better, but also not worse. As the shadows of the day grow long, my patience grows short. I begin to think that the next morning might be a good time to do my own doctoring with some antibiotics. The shaman comes my way and pours the pot of used medicinal plants into the ground. He lights his *mapacho* cigarette, blows tobacco smoke over my infected right toe and commences with the *ícaros* spirit chants. My pharmacist-self is wondering how this ritual could possibly fix my infected toe, but I do appreciate the calmness that overcomes me during these healing rituals.

The next morning upon awakening at dawn with the squawking call of the macaws overhead, I reach out from under my mosquito netting and under my bed for my blue flip-flops—they do not hurt my infected toe. Rubbing the sleep from my eyes, I look down at my feet to put on my flip-flops. To my surprise, I see that my right toe is markedly better, almost healed. How did that happen? Soliciting the guide to help translate for me, we head for the shaman's hut to show him the good news.

"How do you think my toe healed so significantly overnight?" I query the shaman.

"Well, the healing herbal foot baths would have worked just fine, but they take time," he answered. "So, I decided to call in more powerful energy—the Spirits—to help us out. That's what I was doing with the tobacco and song healing, calling in the power of Spirit."

My toe might have healed without the final spiritual healing ritual, of course. But what strikes me in remembering this entire process from beginning to end is that I've I learned four important healing principles—first, the healing power of fresh green medicines; next, the healing power of the love through the "attending physician" principle; third, the healing power of community: and last, but not least, the healing power of Spirit. All four principles are an integral part of the Amazonian shamanic medicine. And the combined effect of all four principles is most certainly a good example of Ecological Medicine—healing in right-relationship with physical, mental and social aspects of our lives.

Health is not merely the absence of disease or infirmity. Health is also the harmony of body-mind-spirit, including our complete interconnectedness and balance with all of life—both the World Health Organization and the jungle shaman agree. The word "shaman" is often loaded with superstition, misinformation, and misunderstandings. Hence, the teachings and medicines of shamans are often suspect. Western Medicine would generally have a hard time with the term "disconnection" as a core root of disease/dis-ease. And most would not even acknowledge the term "Shamanic Medicine". As a medical insider, I find the term Ecological Medicine to be equally powerful and useful, without any loaded interpretation.

13
Right-Relationships that Heal

Loren Cole, who was the Executive Director of our nonprofit organization (Living Amazon Peru) up until the very end of his life—and one of a group of original founders of Earth Day almost 50 years ago—was awarded the only doctorate in Ecosystemology ever granted by University of California, Berkeley. He dedicated his authoritative and impressive life's work to the "whole systems" approach to all things in life. He taught that ecology itself is a systems science of relationships, the dynamics, between groups of living things and their environment.

Our environment is the natural world around us, and includes us. In applying his teachings to the principles of health, I use the term Ecological Medicine to mean the medicine of right-relationship with our environment. Humans are part of a local ecosystem. Disturbed ecosystems can surely make people ill—harmonious ecosystems, likewise, foster life. Our life depends on a healthy environment of all things around us—plants, animals, rivers, people, and the air we breathe.

I pause in my note-taking about all this scientific and medical perspective on health. Rubbing my eyes under the rims of my steamed-up eyeglasses, I begin to see images of my *maestro* giving healings and consultations to western visitors to the jungle. Invariably, they are confused by his diagnoses of "lack of right-relationships" with the people, places and things of their life. As he said to one woman with asthmatic symptoms, "You are allergic to your place of work. You need to change jobs so that you can heal without medication." He means the term "allergic" on every level—physiological, psychological, and spiritual. Interestingly, she not only has an allergy to the new carpet in her office, but she also does not get along with her boss. To another Prozac-resistant case he said, "You are depressed and need to volunteer at your local community garden to get more direct *energia positiva* from nature." A month later, she did just that, and reported back to me that she was pleased to report that her long-standing depression had largely lifted the more she was in nature and community. To me, "Your pain of repetitive stress in your wrists is because you should not be a pharmacist anymore, you have more expansive healing work in the world to do." In a diagnosis, he does not parse out what is wrong with the body as separate from what is wrong with the spirit. Yes, physically

I have carpal tunnel syndrome—which working as a pharmacist exacerbates—as well as spiritually I also have other gifts outside of the knowledge of pharmacy to share with the world. Both the physical and spiritual aspects are true, and my *maestro* sees them as one and the same health issue.

I can attest that in all three cases, his "diagnosis" proved to be correct. Rather than "take a pill", the shaman suggested they "make change in their lives". In these cases, no medication was needed, but the re-establishment of right-relationships in their lives. My *maestro,* with his shamanic/ecological medicine, sees the "wholeness" needed in a person's life—not just only a treatment for the symptoms.

In Western Medical terms there is the field of Environmental Medicine—a multidisciplinary field involving medicine, environmental science, chemistry and biology—overlapping with environmental health. By Environmental Medicine we generally signify that the quality of the environment around us affects our health.

Bad air might give us asthma; bad water might give us bad health conditions caused by contamination from farming and mining run-off; certain animals and plants we eat might give us ill health from the GMOs, hormones and antibiotics they contain. A healthy environment provides us with breathable air, drinkable water, and good uncontaminated food. Ecological Medicine—right-relationship—also must be involved with creating and maintaining healthy environments around us, which support the health of we humans who inhabit and are part of the environment.

Time to summarize my journal notes, as my ballpoint pen is beginning to skip over areas of moist dampness on the page. There is a difference between the term *environment* and the term *ecology*. Ecology is the homeo-dynamic interactions of our environment—trees, rivers, animals—around us, and includes us. The health of humanity is mutually and relationally bound with the health of the environment. Improving the environment improves human health and wellbeing. Ecological Medicine is the medicine of helping to establish balance and harmony—right-relationship—with all that is around us and in us, thus promoting homeo-dynamic health. Ecological Medicine calls all of us to develop a higher ecological consciousness that also includes the care and welfare of Mother Earth—every shaman knows that.

Bottom line, we are not separate. Ulti-mately, perceived or created separateness or disconnectedness is what causes dis-ease and adds to disease. The answer is connection to the greater world around us. The interconnected-ness of all life is a fundamental truth of life itself. We all intuitively know this to be true. I've said this already in so many forms and in so many ways, yet wonder what it will take for us to "get it" in our hearts.

Shadows of the day grow longer, and the dusk brings a pensive mood. My mind begins to contemplate the idea of including the health and wellbeing of the Amazon in our personal equa-tion of the ecological world. I've thought only about my own immediate social network, colleagues, friends and family as being important in my circle of right-relationship for good health and wellbeing. Since I believe "as goes the Amazon, so goes the world", I must now include the ecological wellness of the Amazon into my right-relationship circle of wellness. I realize in the moment, that the *energia positiva* that I experience in my trips to the Amazon is not separate from my healthful life in the San Francisco Bay Area. I now know that my love of the Amazon is also a drive for the preservation of my Self and my Soul—for as goes the Amazon, so do I.

After a long restful day of contemplation and writing, we dine on fleshy white catfish with tart *limón*, red ripe tomatoes, pink *camu camu* juice, and white rice. Plas, the lodge's local naturalist guide, suggests that my friend Peggy and I go for a night boat ride after dinner as the skies are clearing and the southern sky constellations are sure to be in brilliant display. I love being out in the boat in the evenings. The jungle shows yet another side of her sensory beauty. The cacophony of wild night sounds is almost deafening—exotic frogs that sound like hammers hitting nails and laughing women, crickets creaking and strumming a loud symphony, and an occasional night animal grunt or growl.

We motor up the river for a bit, then stop to stargaze. This starry night fills the sky with the upside-down Big Dipper, and the Crux—the Southern Cross. Peggy lies down on the boat seat to get the best view, face-up to the celestial heavens. The Milky Way is beginning to whiten up across the velvety black of the entire night sky, transporting me to dreamy ecstatic thoughts. Stunning. Awesome. All the cliché descriptive words just don't do justice to the experience.

After about an hour of stargazing we begin to motor gently and quietly back down the river toward the lodge. Just where the river begins to narrow to bring the river banks closer to the boat, Plas excitedly points and shouts, "Look there. Look at the concert of fireflies along each river bank!" There were thousands and thousands and thousands of fireflies interlaced among the river bank's trees, all twinkling in concert around us—magical! Each twinkle sparks a dream waiting to happen. Plas is ecstatic himself, you can see it in his star-lit eyes.

I feel like I'm literally being transported into the otherworldliness of the movie *Avatar.* I sense that I'm being dissolved into the magic of the evening's theatrical firefly show, the penetrating vibration of the night sounds, and the expansiveness of the eternity of the sky above.

Peggy turns her head my way and says, "This evening I'm experiencing what I'd call the Eighth Wonder of the World. I've had the wonderful opportunity to experience many things profane and sacred all over the world. This tops it all. It's simply stunning, my dear." She continues to ooooh and ahhhh with delight as though she is watching a fourth of July fireworks display.

She then sits up and faces both Plas and me and continues, "I just now 'got' the importance of the Amazon, why conserving it is important. I've believed intellectually that conserving the Amazon is important, but now I have internalized it. I've internalized it through Plas's passion tonight—the Amazonian people hold this magic of the Amazon in their hearts and being."

Peggy reaches up with both arms to the heavens and out to the fireflies lighting the way and says, "I, too, now want to help conserve all that is precious and all that I love about the Amazon. The Amazon is now in my heart."

It is in this moment that we both internalize, yet ever more deeply, that we are all one with the universe and with the Earth and with its inhabitants—including the Amazon. How could we not be?

14
It's Free for the Taking

The lack of biophilic activities and time spent in nature is creating the disconnection of humans from nature. A lack of connection with the rest of nature fosters disregard for plants, animals and wild spaces. We think of plants, animals, and wild spaces as "other"—not part of ourselves. This disregard leads to further ecosystem degradation. As Jungian psychologist James Hillman warns, "The coming ecological disaster we worry about has already occurred, and goes on occurring. It takes place in the accounts of ourselves that separate ourselves from the world."

Spend more time in nature, as my *maestro* urges. It is in nature that you will be healed.

I am sitting in a rosewood hand-carved deck chair on the deck of my *apartamento* in Iquitos, the mesmerizing view of the Amazon River luring me into a meditative reverie. It is after dinner and growing dark. The sights and sounds of the colorful and frenzied Iquitos working-harbor are dying down. All this writing and con-templation about nature-as-healer over these past weeks and months keeps calling me even deeper into the nature of Nature. I keep mulling over my shamanic teachings from my *maestro* and other-worldly experiences I've had such as the Spirit Doctors apparitions of my apprentice-ship, and how all this relates to the modern world of science and medicine. How to translate and make sense of other-worldly experiences in order to teach others is a challenge.

Around 8:30pm I make a final cup of tea before bedtime, and resume my comfortable deck chair perch. The twinkling stars above hypnotize me. In my deepening sleep reverie, I begin to see the faint outlines of the Spirit Doctors—two of them, always a man and a woman. I've long been fascinated by their healing abilities and amazed at their remarkable appearance in healings sessions I give others. Yet I am puzzled as to who or what these entities really are. *Who are these Spirit Doctors?*—the question burns itself into my mind as I drift off to sleep.

After some deep sleep the Spirit Doctors suddenly appeared as a puff of clouds and a mass of swirling energy.

"You called for us?" they asked, as if genies being summoned from a lamp.

"Yes," I answer. "I'm curious. Exactly who and what are you? How can I, how should I, explain you to others?"

"We are the sheer unbridled healing forces of Nature that you, as a shamana, are learning to harness and call upon for the sake of others," they bellow in clear deep voices. "It is we, the generative forces of Nature, who do the healing. Not you."

With that, they slip away. And so do I, into the depths of a sound sleep.

I awaken alert with a lot of *energia positiva,* positive energy, to greet the day. With a strong cup of *café con leche,* I eagerly attack the growing stack of journals, notes and books on the subject of nature I've accumulated. I want to pull together the nuggets of truth from all of them. These research factoids about the wellness gifts of nature are especially for the scientists, healthcare professionals, and the show-me-the-evidence folks.

What does it take to heal? I write these words in big letters across the top of the first page of my journal. In the larger sense, healing is thought of as different than curing. Curing is the restoration of health—the physical disease or symptoms are gone. Healing, as every shaman knows, restores us to wholeness— mental, emotional, and spiritual wellbeing.

A healing does not necessarily include treatment of the physical condition. The shaman seeks both for their patients, the healing and the curing.

Nature heals us. I often give a scientific lecture on the Healing Power of Nature. According to research, modern life can disrupt our connection to nature, but green spaces improve our health. Being in nature or even viewing scenes of nature, balances our autonomic system, reducing the fight-or-flight response. Interestingly, the Japanese have long had a practice called "forest bathing", just being present in a forest. Research results on "forest bathing" show that forest environments promote lower levels of cortisol, lower pulse rate, lower blood pressure, and a more balanced sympathetic nervous system activity than do city environments. When I've complained to my *maestro* about the effects of the stressors of my life in modern America, my *maestro* says to me, "Just take two brief breaks every day out in nature. Let the sunshine, good air, and the sight and sounds and smells of nature do their work." It is just that simple.

Nature soothes us and helps us cope with pain. As a healthcare professional I am well aware of the research studies that show that patients in hospital settings with views of nature tolerate pain better, have fewer negative effects, take less medication, and tally a shorter hospital stay. My own wrist repetitive stress syndrome all but vanishes whenever I'm in the jungle, even while deep in the throes of writing this book here in the Amazon.

Nature restores us. Nature impacts our sense of well-being. Spending time outdoors results in a positive mood, psychological wellbeing, meaningfulness, and vitality. We shift from depressed, stressed, and anxious feelings to a more calm, relaxed, and balanced sense of Self. I see and feel the shift in everyone who comes to the Amazon on group trips with me deep into the jungle. The day after they arrive everyone's eyes shine bright, like flashlights filled with the light of deep nature's life-force.

Time in nature increases our ability to pay attention. Nature is a respite for our overactive minds, the dis-ease of modern life. Nature refreshes us for new tasks ahead such as reading a book, doing our job, and attending to life's many needs. A friend of mine who is a final year medical resident, and her husband who is diagnosed with ADHD, visited me in the Amazon a few years ago. She commented that her husband's focus greatly improves when he is in nature. I told her about the research on green therapy and ADHD which shows that time in nature reduces the symptoms, and that exposure to the greenest settings improves attention the best. She already knew about the study, and commented that the same positive results also hold true for non-ADHD individuals exposed to nature.

Nature connects us. Time spent in nature connects us to each other and the larger world. When we are in nature, parts of the brain associated with empathy and love light up. Nature inspires feelings that connect us to each other and our environment. Our existential fears fade away as we expand into a connectedness with the greater universe around us. When I am in a cosmopolitan area anywhere in the world, my mind wanders more easily to the anxieties of life in general. Yet, when I sit out on the deck of the Iquitos *apartmento* overlooking the Amazon River most evenings, I feel at-one with the nature that surrounds me—I feel a part of this grand universe. Existential anxieties all but disappear.

Nature has a soul, according to noted psychiatrist Carl Gustav Jung. Jung spoke and wrote extensively about his concern about humanity's loss of connection with nature. "People get dirty through too much civilization. Whenever we touch nature, we get clean," comments Jung. A Jungian psychologist friend of mine, a nature mystic herself, added that Jung considered nature to be the "nourishing soil of the soul". Jung's wise words strike me as the central gold nugget to the alchemical synthesis of the modern ecologist and the ancient shaman.

From nature-based Jungian principles, to healthcare research, and now on to the Church, we learn from a wide variety of paradigms of the importance of nature. We hear our current Pope Francis commenting on the need for more nature in our modern lives. "Nature is filled with words of love," Pope Francis states, "but how can we listen to them amid constant noise, interminable and nerve-wracking distractions, or the cult of appearances?" He goes on to boldly comment, "For many, nature can be a church." I welcome this quote with gratitude and applause, one of Pope Francis's many now-famous green quotes.

I am gently reminded of the first day of my shamanic apprenticeship deep in the jungles of the Amazon when my *maestro* instructed me, "The healing is in the sights and the sounds and the smells of nature." It took me many years of apprenticeship to "get" the profundity of what he meant—this simple yet profound truth.

This jungle shaman's simple assertion about the powerful benefits of nature is in harmony with the best and most respected minds and institutions. And after a multitude of years of apprenticeship with this shaman, I now understand his statement and believe it to be true.

Nature is also a source of spirit. Shamanism is based on the teachings of the earth, of direct communication with nature. By communicating and learning from the plants and animals, from the rocks and mountains, from the winds and waters, and from the sun, moon, and stars, shamans use the power of nature for survival and knowledge. Shamans also work with the spirits of nature for healing and power. Beyond the apparition sense of spirit, by the "spirit of nature" I mean the force within all of nature that gives life, energy, and power.

Nature is a huge source of power for shamans. Indigenous shamans seek the sanctuary of nature often. In fact, nature is where the shaman gets super-charged with natural energy.

Think about it—where else, but from nature it-self, would impoverished shamans worldwide obtain all the spiritual power they are known to possess? No need to take a thousand-dollar workshop on shamanism, or to buy a library of books on shamanism, unless you want to. All the power a shaman needs—or all of us, for that matter—is directly under their feet, overhead and all around them, and it's free for the taking.

I believe that all of us have the ability to tap into the power of nature to help heal ourselves and unlock the shaman's secret—*and it's free!*

15
Reciprocidad

Back in the U.S. for a short six-week stay, I'm stateside just long enough to give a brief lecture tour on the topic of higher spiritual principles that glue the matrix of existence together. As quantum physics teaches us, the universe is interactive. Perennial philosophies hold this basic tenet to be true, indigenous peoples of the past and present practice it as a way of life, yet we modern people have largely forgotten the powerful ways of this principle. But I believe that for all of us, it's not too late to remember this practice and our place in the interactive creation of the universe in which we live.

I call the San Francisco Bay Area "the largest ashram in the world". By that I mean that where I live in the Bay Area there is an enormous number of spiritual practices from various world traditions available by which to gain wisdom. As I begin to organize my thoughts for writing an outline and topic title for these tour talks, I tap into my own Whitman's Sampler of spiritual principles I have learned from over the years. The overarching principle is reciprocity—the interactive physical and spiritual life we co-create with the universe.

For example, there are many forms of sacred reciprocity—such as *Seva, Prasad,* Giveaways, *Ayni, Reciprocidad*—that have always been part of various spiritual beliefs and practices throughout the world. In Hindu religion, *Seva* is selfless service volunteer work. It's about turning compassion into action for the betterment of all. Ram Dass ardently impressed this important principle of *Seva* upon his audience at one of his many Bay Area appearances.

The Sanskrit word *Prasad* means the gracious gift of selfless service. Gurumayi of the Siddha Yoga tradition taught us, at one of her Oakland Ashram talks, that *Prasad* is created by a process of giving and receiving. A dramatic experience of the principle of Prasad happened to me in a Siddha Yoga Ashram in South Fallsburg, New York. I traveled to the Ashram specifically to meet Gurumayi. Upon first arriving, we were all assigned a selfless service project—mine was to work in the kitchen. Day after day, I peeled sacks of white potatoes, made innumerable batches of coffee in the samovar, and cleaned mountains of dirty dishes.

One afternoon, while washing the lunchtime dishes, it happened. My back was to the door, my arms up to my elbows in sudsy water, when suddenly I experienced multiple waves of ecstatic rapture ripple through my body. I turned around to see what was going on in the kitchen, and there in the doorway stood Gurumayi herself. She looked at me straight in the eyes, flashed her famous Mona Lisa smile, and seemed to silently say to me, "I bless you with the *shaktipat,* spiritual energy, of selfless service. Thank you for your *Prasad.*"

In the Native American tradition, generosity is a religious act as well as a social one. A widely-practiced ceremony, a Giveaway, is held to redistribute a person's possessions within the community. This is often done as a potlatch, a gift-giving feast, where property and gifts are ceremonially distributed. I participated in my first potlatch Giveaway at a powerful sweat lodge in Sebastopol many years ago. At first, I thought the Giveaway was simply a nice-thing-to-do-at-the-end-of-a-ritual. I was taught otherwise by the Elders facilitating the sweat lodge. They informed me that Native American indigenous reciprocity is not just a philosophical principle, but rather a way of life. The idea is that in life we are guests on this land, not owners. Our relationship to natural resources must be sustainable because we are all part of a cosmic hospitality system of give and take.

Ayni is a similar concept that refers to the concept of reciprocity among Andean mountain people—the Quechuas, Aymaras, and other tribes that live in Ecuador, Bolivia, and Peru. Their principle belief and commandment of daily life is that everything in the world is connected—*Ayni*. *Ayni* also refers to the cooperation and reciprocity between the members of a community—if you do or give something to one member, then you are entitled to receive something back. *Ayni* also refers to the exchange of energy between humans, nature, and the universe—I learned this firsthand in Bolivia some time ago. *Ayni* can be as simple an act as watering a tree, then the tree gives shade and fruit back to the human. Ayni is their ordinal truth, and is regarded as the most important principle as it provides the backbone of life. We can all learn from this, it is not too late.

Nothing would exemplify the working principles of the exchange of energy between humans, nature, and the spirit of the universe more than a profound personal experience in the Altiplano region of Bolivia, between La Paz and Lake Titicaca. The backstory is that in Bolivia I was working for Aveda on a plant fragrance project that required me to work closely with an Aymara shaman named Rufino. For weeks I had been following him everywhere to obtain the information I needed for Aveda. When following a shaman, for any reason, there are always many rituals to participate in along the way. We performed several *despachos* each week—*despacho* means "to send" an offering—and *coca* rituals several times a day, including *coca* blessings of each trail and river we crossed along our treks. Not knowing anything about the Quechua traditions, since my time spent and rituals experienced have largely been of the Amazonian jungle tradition, I simply followed Rufino's instructions and mimicked his actions.

At the end of our Aveda assignments, we decided to treat ourselves to a few days of relaxation at a natural mineral spa high in the Andes. Relaxed and refreshed, on the last day of our stay we opted to take ourselves and a picnic basket even higher up the mountainside to lunch at a flat clearing and enjoy the spectacular view.

Sated by the delicious lunch, the mesmerizing Andean mountain views, and in an altered state due to the lack of oxygen in the high altitude, I was lulled into a reverie trance. Suddenly I was shocked awake by the presence of a towering human-like spirit.

Recovering myself a few moments later, I asked, "Who are you?"

"I am the great Wiracocha, god of creation of the Inca tradition," answered the great booming voice.

Surprised at the response, I questioned further, "To what do I owe the honor of your visit?"

"My dear, you have performed many traditional rituals to honor my people and my land. You have given of your heart and spirit. You may now do business in Bolivia." Then the great spirit of Wiracocha faded into the ethers.

Eighteen months later, due to this *Ayni* reciprocity exchange, I was easily able to get placement of a Bolivian natural *maca* product into all of the health-food stories in Canada. Although I had been diligently working with the Bolivian manufacturer and the Canadian distributor for some time, I had been doubtful that much would happen due to strict Canadian herb-labeling laws and import regulations. I am thoroughly convinced that the Andean Inca principle of *Ayni* was at work, and largely responsible for this quick and successful business transaction.

Six months later, I learn firsthand about the power of the Amazon tradition of *Reciprocidad,* reciprocity. One especially clear Amazon day at my *maestro's* humble *tambo* deep in the forest, the river and sky gods are both wearing the same shade of glistening aquamarine blue. My *maestro* and I are enjoying an afternoon break and a tall glass of water.

Through my water glass, I see what looks like yet another shellac-brown *cucaracha*, cockroach, crawling along the dirt floor of his hut. He reads my mind and says, "It's not a *cucaracha*. It's a baby scarab beetle, it has no horns yet." He reaches down and tenderly picks up the little creature, bringing it outside the hut where it is then free to go, giving it safety and life.

"I will now teach you the secret of the shamans—how to get more power," my *maestro* says. He leans in and cups his hand around his mouth and my ears, "You have to make deals with the Spirits. It's called *Reciprocidad*."

Pulling back a bit so I can look him in the eyes, I assert, "The Spirits are already asking me for reciprocity—to make deals with them." I recount the dream story of the Spirit Doctors giving me the specific instructions—We will continue to be with you for your clients and your work if you agree to continue bringing people into Nature.

"Yes," he says, "You now know that sacred *Reciprocidad* is the secret to the power of life itself."

16
River's Breath

From our very own first breath we were all
brought forth into this beautiful world. Breath is
life. Our lungs fuel us with oxygen, the body's
life-sustaining gas. With our first breath of life,
we are born into the consciousness of this world
we know. May we continue to become more conscious of the world around us with each continuing breath we take.

An American eco-tourist and I are walking
along a canopy-occluded dark jungle trail deep
in the forest behind the popular Heliconia

Amazon River Lodge. Under the forest canopy, the sunlight is mottled against the ferns and other low growth that marks our way. A group of four tiny brown ring-tailed pygmy marmoset monkeys—any one of them could fit the palm of my hand—startle us with their incessant trilling and babbling as they playfully scamper from branch to branch across our path. We're in a wonderland of a myriad of small yellow butterflies, long dripping-red heliconias, and purple trumpet-like flowers raining down from the jacaranda tree overhead.

In the meditative silence of the jungle hike, the in-tune eco-tourist turns to me, inhales deeply and says, "I feel like I'm being breathed...ahhhhh. I hardly have to effort at all to inhale and exhale in this oxygen-rich environment."

We step into the clearing that marks the beginning of the medicinal plant trail. I pause to wipe my brow, as it's always humid and close under the canopy.

"Yes, your senses are right," I respond. "The Amazon's nickname is the 'Lungs of the World' because it pumps vast amounts of oxygen into the atmosphere and removes huge amounts of carbon. We continue to rely on the Amazon for our continuing daily breath. The Amazon is aptly called the 'Lungs of the World' as it supplies 20% of the world's oxygen—*breathe*."

Back at the lodge, over a dinner of *chonta* (heart of palm salad) and sumptuous sweet *paiche* fish, we continue to talk about both the beauty of the Amazon and the environmental dilemmas it faces. Finishing her last forkful of salad, she anxiously concludes, "I get that the Amazon rainforest stores carbon and gives us oxygen in return. So why, exactly, are we cutting it down?"

17
Flying River

The *flying river,* as it's known, is a movement of large quantities of water vapor transported in the atmosphere from the Amazon Basin to other parts of South America. The forest trees release water vapor into the atmosphere through transpiration and this moisture is deposited in other parts of South America in the form of precipitation. In reality, while standing in a jungle clearing and looking up to the heavens, there is an invisible virtual sky-river overhead—incredible!

One late evening after my favorite succulent *paiche* fish dinner, I retire to my room to write in my personal journal. I'm inspired by the many and always-deepening thoughts and insights from my day in the jungle. I often do my best writing and thinking in the Amazon, definitely my muse. The wooden boards creek under my feet as I walk down the wooden corridor to my quarters. As I reach for the doorknob, I hear thunder in the distance.

As I glance up into the black inky sky for some sign of impending weather, I notice a slow-moving hairy black tarantula up in the rafters. Tarantulas are the biggest spiders on Earth, and the largest 13-inch leg-span tarantulas are found in the Amazon. I wonder for a moment if the spider has something to tell me. Or might she be an omen, the hairs standing up on my forearm, for what is to come. The intense energies of the impending storm this evening are spiritually electrifying.

Entering my room, I flip the switch by the door to take advantage of the last of the lodge's solar electricity captured from what was a typical sunny jungle day. As I sharpen my pencil with my Swiss Army knife—call me old-fashioned, I love the feel of lead pushing across my journal paper—I ponder the day and its teachings.

Somewhere earlier that day I found an interesting factoid in a left-over city newspaper. I had saved the article to reread the science and statistics portion, to understand it fully. Unfolding it now from my backpack and smoothing out the creases, I read again the interesting fact that a big jungle tree with a crown of roughly 60-feet across evaporates about 80 gallons a day. That's a lot of water for just one tree. How much for a whole forest, I wonder. The chart in the paper explains that one square meter of ocean evaporates only one square meter (about 264 gallons) of water. To compare, one square meter of forest can contain about ten meters of leaves, so it evaporates about ten times more (2640 gallons more) than the ocean. The article goes on to conclude that this means the "flying river" rising into the atmosphere in the form of vapor, is bigger than the biggest river on Earth.

Just then, an electrifying lightning bolt and deafening clap of thunder grab my attention. I furtively glance up to the brown overlay of thatched roof. Will it hold? There's nothing like the power of one of these big *tormentas,* jungle storms. As I put pencil to thankfully dry paper, my mind snaps into a higher consciousness, as if jolted from reality by the storm. I get it now. While I'm no meteorologist, my heart-mind sharpens to grasp the full meaning of the dynamics of these life-giving flying rivers and the fate of the Amazon.

I fold up this newspaper article into fours and stick it between the pages of my journal. I scribble some final notes to myself, hurrying to finish before the rains begin, just in case the electricity goes out in the storm. The Amazon rainforest, acting as a gigantic hydraulic pump, spreads humidity from the trees through the air and guarantees irrigation of the region. That vital role is diminishing due to deforestation.

A lack of flying rivers, vapor clouds from the Amazon that carry rain, is also drying up rivers and reservoirs in other parts of South America. Everyone and everything everywhere suffers then from the lack of water.

Until now, I don't think I actually "got" all of the ecology and sustainability information as one unified dynamic. I understood with my head, but not with the whole of my heart. After twenty-five years of apprenticing in the jungles of the Amazon, I now realize I'm still apprenticing to the soul of the Amazon. I believe she still has life-giving secrets to share and lessons to teach all of us.

18
What's It Worth to You?

We value things because of their worth to us.
How do we measure the worth of the Amazon?
What's the bottom line—what is the Amazon
worth to us?

It's my 60th birthday, and I am excited to
celebrate it deep in the jungles of the Amazon
with a handful of high-powered business friends
and heart-powered personal friends from the
United States. One of these good friends is
Jonathan, an investor based on the East Coast
who travels globally looking for promising

investments in the insurance industry. Personally, he has deep concern for what humankind is/is-not willing do—to invest in—to insure the sustainability of the Amazon, with all of its gifts of nature.

Now settled into the lodge and our rich jungle experience, Jonathan announces out of the clear blue, "I'm not really on vacation, it seems to me I've been invited to a business board meeting conducted by the Great Powers of Nature."

I see with my mind's eye an invisible lightbulb going on over his head. He emphatically punctuates to catch our attention, "The Great Powers of Nature have called this meeting, and mandated that I attend!"

Jonathan's comments set the tone for the afternoon's conversations. Just after lunch and before hammock-*siesta* time, Jonathan and I get into a discussion about how to raise the consciousness of the importance of the Amazon to us all.

Jonathan starts with, "First off, people need to know, to understand, to feel the 'worth' of the Amazon, or they won't be compelled to act to save the Amazon."

We are still sitting at the dining room table, finishing off the pitcher of thirst-quenching mango juice. "Pure ambrosia," I say with satisfaction as I down the last refreshing swallow.

"People always talk about the 'bottom line', about profit or loss, with the belief that a business can only be sustainable if it is profitable," begins Jonathan. "But when you look at the Amazon, that profit-loss thinking is limited. It's necessary to think much more broadly—similar to what people used to talk about as the Triple Bottom Line, or TBL."

Another business-oriented friend joins in the animated discussion. Pete, with his diverse social work, post-grad business degrees, and decades of work experience, adds, "That TBL analogy is correct. The Triple Bottom Line, is made up of three elements, or 'Ps' of business— Profit, People, and Planet. Profit accounts for the financial side of things; People are attended through social aspects; and the Planet is taken care of with environmental considerations. These three Ps of TBL are the essence of sustainability, and are ascertained by measuring the impact of an organization's activities on the world. Ultimately, this means that business success is no longer defined only by monetary gain but also by the impact an organization's activities have on society as a whole."

Wow. I think as my mind reels out its own silent chatter. Pete, with his dual degrees in social work and business, is himself a model of interdisciplinary ethics for the greater good of the world and its inhabitants. This is going to be a grounded, detailed, business conversation—I can tell. I'm rarely around business people when I am in the Amazon. But after years of my own experience in bridging the business and spiritual worlds—and with a master's degree in non-profit public administration—I'm equally comfortable in each.

"There is now a Quadruple Bottom Line or QBL which includes the fourth P, representing Purpose or meaning," I chime in. "This additional parameter allows for transcendence and takes the equation even higher." I gesture with open palms rising, pressing each finger of one open hand for each concept. I add quickly and emphatically, "It is radically higher because it includes the concepts of ethics, culture, intergenerational equity, social justice, inner values and spirituality."

I slide my chair closer to the table to command more attention, as my thoughts continue to flow. "The QBL recognizes deeper notions of human meaning, of considerations beyond just ourselves. It shifts us from an economy focus on what we *could* do, towards an economy based on what we *should* do."

As we sit there quietly, thinking about the impact of this concept, I can see that this concept of QBL has real wisdom and power. I summed up what we are all thinking, "By moving in this direction, more emphasis is placed on the wisdom of inner values and a purposeful life and generational sustainability."

It is now well after 2:00 in the afternoon, the time when the jungle is warming up to the high heat of the day. As Jonathan gets up from his dining room chair, he comments on the richness of the jungle flora and fauna scenes hand-carved into the beautiful red-brown rosewood chairs and bar front. We all saunter together out of the dining room and into the hammock house at the river's edge where it's much cooler.

I take a comfy rosewood slatted deck chair. Jonathan finds an empty hammock and sits in it sideways with his legs dangling so we can continue the conversation eye-to-eye. Pete is quick to take the last available hammock for himself.

"When we talk about 'people' as being one of the four factors of sustainability," Jonathan adds to my previous comments, "we include the concepts of health, vigor, wellbeing, flourishing, and a good quality of life. 'Profit' means competitive productivity in producing and distributing goods and services for consumption. Profit, with scarce resources, should mean using our resources wisely for the benefit of all."

Jonathan's ease and facility with this business language and topic indicates he has given this talk before at many board meetings across the globe. He's on a roll.

"Good for the 'planet' encompasses sustainable ecosystems for individual, community and ecosystems survival across lifespans and generations," Jonathan continues.

"The fourth P," Jonathan restates, "stands for 'purpose' in our QBL framework. Purpose includes the higher principles of personal meaning, inner values, and spirituality. Answering to a QBL means developing ways of living and ways of creating wealth that value being rather than having." He points to the heavens, "The Great Powers of Nature know that it is possible to have profits without plunder."

I can see now why Jonathan's first global business was called Katalyst—a catalyst being an agent that provokes or speeds significant change and action. Jonathan, from that potent dynamic of change, speaks with power with humility. He expects more than just profit, in that profit must be taken in the context of sustainability for future generations.

With all this intense conversation, I offer up a practical consideration, "Beyond this theoretical consideration of concepts, I will ask the big question—what is the Amazon really worth?"

In my excited and inspired state, I pace the hammock house floor unable to sit still. Neither a chair nor a hammock is of interest to me at the moment. I look first to Pete, who is good with figures.

Pete puts forth expertly, "I suppose if we consider the worth of the Amazon only through the narrow lens of the old profit/loss concept, the Amazon is worth only the value of the resources we can harvest from it to sell in the marketplace."

Pete summons the lodge manager and the local staff and asks for some rough local prices. He jots them into his notebook, and quickly throws some figures together.

"For a local jungle farmer, for the sake of this conversation," Pete continues, "this rainforest land here converted to cattle operations yields the farmer $60 per acre. If the plentiful timber on his land is also sold outright, his land is worth almost $400 per acre."

"But," Pete adds, doing a bit more math-on-the-fly, "by adding some of the QBL principles of environmental sustainability, such as renewable timber and other local sustainable resources to be harvested and sold, in just a few years the land could yield the landowner...hmmm...up to $2,400 per acre."

Plop. Splat. A blur of something green and wet just dropped onto the floor between our hammocks. Now that it has landed and our eyes could focus, we can see that it is a small green vine snake with a frog in its mouth. The snake must have lost its balance in catching its prey and plummeted to the floor. These green vine snakes slither through branches and sometimes palm roofs in search of food. This 24-inch skinny snake continues holding onto the head of the sizable frog, even with all the human commotion surrounding him.

Everybody and everything stops. Our eyes are glued to the scene and the snake is holding completely still, waiting for the frog to stop twitching. Then, unhitching its jaws, the small snake manages to swallow the frog whole in one bite. We all watch the bulge in the snake's body as the eaten frog slowly moves down to the center portion of the snake. After a few moments, the snake with whole frog inside slithers out of the hammock house and up to a tree branch to rest and digest its lunch. Nothing like nature in the raw to ground our cerebral conversation, I think to myself.

Jonathan repositions himself in his hammock, his mind as expansive as the 30-foot-high thatched roof above.

"If we add in more QBL principles to the concept of the Amazon as 'the greatest expression of life on Earth', then beyond the world of dollars-and-cents, we must take into account an amazing array of flora and fauna. The Amazon rainforest contains the largest collection of living plant and animal species in the world."

Reaching over to an Amazon photo-and-fact reference book at a table next to his hammock, Jonathan opens to the "Riches of the Amazon" section.

"It says here that an acre in the Amazon produces up to 250 species of trees, and 600 species of higher plants," he continues, "The Amazon rainforests produce 20% of the world's oxygen, and its rivers hold one-fifth of the world's fresh water—the necessities of life itself."

Jonathan turns the page and continues his staccato bulleted-reading, "The number of species of fish in the Amazon exceeds the number found in the entire Atlantic Ocean. The blue Amazon skies are home to one-in-five of all the birds in the world. To date, more than 400,000 species of plants of economic and social interest have been registered in the region, to become new pharmaceuticals for some of mankind's most intractable diseases. And, lest we forget, the Amazon rainforests are also home to some 7500 species of butterflies."

Pausing long enough to take in a deep breath, looking up from his book, Jonathan peers directly into our eyes. He slaps his palm down upon the red book cover, as if to wake us up to the truth at hand.

Jonathan then emphatically implores, "The Amazon rainforests are known as the 'Jewels of the Earth'. What price...what worth...what value...I ask all of you, shall we put upon this veritable Garden of Eden?"

Why do all these hard, cold facts make my head hurt? I love being in the expansive pure life-giving energy of the jungle. But all this difficult-to-hear information makes me feel anxious. My morning mango juice has soured in my stomach. I purposefully shift my thoughts away from my stomach and onto my heart.

During our intense discussion on the value of the Amazon—an Amazonian Board Meeting!—I take up occupancy in an empty woven hammock and join him in his thousand-mile stare up the high conical thatched roof. Pete gazes out over the river, beyond the lush green forest, into the deep blue horizon, giving Amazon Mother Nature her due. What value, I ponder, shall we put on the quintessential poster child of the Amazon—the Blue Morpho butterfly—that suddenly flutters before us? Its glistening prismatic-blue wings the size of coffee-cup saucers navigate past me on their drunken path toward a lunch of fruit juice and tree sap. The heavens must have opened up, just this very moment, to allow one Blue Morpho to escape the celestial realms for our earthly pleasure, and to grace our day.

My heart wants to know the value of the giant Victoria Regia water lilies, named after Queen Victoria, that are native to the oxbow lakes and the shallow backwaters of the Amazon. I feel like an intruder spying on private moments as I see indigenous women using these gigantic floating Victoria Regia lily pads, up to three meters wide, as river bassinets upon which to bathe their precious babies. What price? My soul aches to know.

Looking overhead at a flock—yes an entire flock—of squawking macaws, my mind's eye interprets rainbows of colors as they streak in flight across the sky. Looking like a flock of "living" rainbows—rainbows in living flesh— I see smears of yellow, red, blue and green pigmentation overhead, an artist's palette in the heavens above. Swooning in the splendor of the moment, I don't want these visions and experiences to stop. Ever.

Would I, could I, live without the daily 5:30am reveille of a howler monkey's deep-throated multi-tonal howls, reminiscent of Siberian Tuva Throat chanting? Rescued from certain death in a soup pot, this howler lives with a group of other monkeys across from the lodge. Every morning he greets the day at sunrise with his low bellowing, the piercing loudness of his howl is certain to awaken most jungle creatures. It just wouldn't be time to get up without his daily morning insistence. The heavenly gods have certainly given him the earthly task of greeting the day.

Tell me, what is the worth of a midnight visit to the deepest parts of the jungle to reach a breathtakingly brilliant constellation of glowing lights upon the ground, a carpet of bioluminescent leaves illuminating the jungle path below my feet? I pick up a handful of these glowing leaves, paste each one on my sweaty arms and legs, fling my arms wide and dance freely in circles, imagining myself aglow as Tinker Bell in this jungle wonderland of magic.

After a good long time in each of our own mental spaces, Jonathan is the first to speak. "The worth of the Amazon depends on who you're talking to—lumber poachers talk about the value of trees on the black market, Big

Pharma talks about the value of the medicinal plants as new drugs, and the indigenous people talk about the value of fish and melons as food."

I quickly add, "I talk about the overwhelming healing power of deep nature. The scientist in me talks about the value of the Amazon because it's the greatest expression of the flora and fauna of life on Earth. The shaman in me talks about the worth of the Amazon as the greatest spiritual experience on Earth, filled with wonderment, awe and magic."

"As goes the Amazon, so do we all," Jonathan concludes. "We all have to do something to help its viability."

Why don't we conserve the Amazon? Have we grown fatigued, hearing "save the Amazon" messages time and time again? What will it take? "Nature lost its divinity for us in these modern days," Carl Gustav Jung once stated. Has the world become disenchanted for us?

Do we not care about the charm, magic and enchantment of the rainbow macaws, the giant Amazon water-lily bassinets, the howler monkey jungle alarm clock, the bioluminescent leaves of the jungle, or the delightful flutter of the Blue Morpho butterfly?

I recall my *maestro's* simple yet profound statement, "The change has to happen inside first. We must care in our hearts first before we have the strength to help the world." I believe he's right. We don't have the drive to save, or better said—conserve—that which we don't value. If we value enough and truly love something, then we will indeed go to great lengths to keep it safe and keep it alive and thriving. I believe we should, and can, and will do this for the Amazon.

If the Amazon is the greatest expression of life on Earth, the greatest concentration of nature's gifts; if nature heals, and deep nature heals more deeply; if the root of all disease/dis-ease is disconnection, and connection to life itself is greatest in the Amazon—one

of the most precious resources on our planet—
then you will find the core answer to what ails
you in body, mind and spirit awaiting you, deep
in the Amazon.

19
Stealing Your Power

Modern life—the distractions of consumerism, bright lights, busy lives—steals our power. It is ubiquitous and insidious. How does it happen? Let me share with you a simple, yet powerful story.

One last day in Iquitos before I head back to California. It always takes me a while to adjust from "jungle time"—everything in its own good time—to civilization time, where everything and everyone is going pell-mell. There's talk on the street that there's a Northern Peru Shaman Conference being held at the Iquitos outdoor stadium. Curious, and with some time to kill, I hail a *motokar* and head to the event already in progress.

When I arrive at the stadium there are mostly empty bleachers, tiered rows of benches, and a center wooden platform with a speaker's table and a standing microphone. It's break time and everyone is milling around, using the facilities, kicking up dirt and kicking up tall shamanic tales to impress each other. This gives me time to wind my way through the bleachers to find a seat somewhere in the empty top rows without interrupting.

Before long a man in a long white, gold-and-blue-embroidered, robe with matching cap walks—or shall I say, struts—toward the standing microphone. The speaker's table fills quickly with three men in ordinary garb, slacks and simple dress shirts. There is one empty chair left at the table. I wonder if there's another speaker to come.

The officiant shaman at the microphone begins. "*Buenos días*. I am don Augustin Rivas."
He rolls the "r" of his name for a full five seconds
for effect. Posturing with outstretched arms, he
continues, "Welcome to the first Northern Peru
Shaman Conference."

While he goes on with his opening remarks,
I scan the audience. Some two hundred
attendees, mostly men, are here. I assume they
are largely Peruvian working shamans, dressed
in modest jeans and well-worn shirts. Very few
gringos in attendance, it's obviously a local
event. Augustin, on the other hand, is regaled in
flowing robes and decked with layers of beads
and amulets—the whole shamanic-nine-yards.

Augustin continues his speech with the
usual lingo of a first conferences, "May this conference be the first of many more to come."

From the side, a man walks quietly onto the
podium. He's wearing simple jeans, cowboy
boots, a straw cowboy hat, and is carrying a
briefcase. Hmmm...a briefcase, how odd.

From his attire, I assume he's a shaman from the coast of Peru. He takes the empty seat.

"May the shamans of northern Peru unite, and learn from each other," Augustin pontificates, gesticulates and postures at the microphone.

The cowboy shaman slowly opens his briefcase on the table. One by one, he even more slowly takes out various artifacts and places them around his tan leather briefcase for all to see. I watch closely and wonder what these ten items could be. My mind wanders from the speaker, and I begin imagining that these items from this man's briefcase could all be part of his holy altar—maybe a sacred *idolo* or two, some tobacco, a macaw feather, holy water, perhaps a small knife. I can't really see what they are. I squint my eyes in hopes of getting a better look from my bleacher seat in the heavens. I suppose this man, this latecomer, is one of the next shaman speakers and is gathering his accoutrements.

Augustin's robes are blowing in the wind, flapping and wrapping and unwrapping themselves from around the microphone stand. He's still speaking his long-winded opening remarks, but the words fade into the background as I grow more curious by the minute about this cowboy shaman's supposed holy altar items. My imagination is in full tilt "supposing" many scenarios.

The next thing I observe, much to my surprise, is the cowboy shaman putting each item one-by-one sloooowly back into the briefcase. Hmmm...curiouser and curiouser. He hasn't even yet spoken to the crowd. Maybe these items are not his holy altar after all. But what could they be? My peripheral vision senses the audience growing squirmy, wiggling in their seats, at the lengthy Augustin speech.

I, too, adjust my posture in the no-back bleacher seat. I re-focus on the events transpiring at the podium and speaker's table. Suddenly, I smack the palm of my right hand against my forehead. I get it—the cowboy shaman is stealing the power of the speaker. With all of Augustin's elaborate shaman's robes and flowery speech, this simply clad cowboy shaman with his briefcase and silent theatrics is cleverly grabbing the audience's attention away from the speaker. No one is paying attention to Augustin. I know I haven't been listening to him for the past fifteen minutes. I've been completely absorbed by the quiet behavior of the cowboy shaman at the table. Gotcha!

Aha! That's how it's done. A living example of stealing someone's power is unfolding right in front of me. The cowboy shaman's distracting movements of putting out "goods on display", in this case his holy altar artifacts, resonate in the back of my head like the fascination with the brightly colored objects of commercialism in the stores. Distraction sneaks up on us.

As I stated earlier, modern life—the distractions of consumerism, bright lights and busy lives—steals your power. If you let it. It's ubiquitous and insidious. Could it be happening right under each of our noses while we are oblivious?

20
The Power of a Shaman Is Their Work in the World

Rufino is an Aymara shaman of the Bolivian *Altiplano,* high planes of the Andes Mountains. I have the pleasure of working with this Bolivian Aymara shaman because of a fortuitous consulting assignment in La Paz.

Rufino says to me, with a twinkle in his eye, "The power of a shaman is known by their work in the world," as he is preparing the weekly *despacho* burning ritual. In Spanish, the word *despacho* literally means "dispatch", thus sending off your prayers to the higher powers that be in the higher heavens above. I have come to learn that a *despacho* is a gift to spirit, and a ritual of energetic exchange, for healing and protection. It re-establishes right-relationship by aligning personal energies with the cosmic energies.

Rufino, in his rough-woven brown alpaca tunic, is seriously busy arranging various symbolic offerings to put into the *despacho* paper, all to be burned in a sacred fire.

"Did you hear what I just said?" Rufino asks as he sprinkles red and white flower petals, corn kernels, shells, sparkly magic trinkets, candies, and coca leaves over a shrunken pale dehydrated llama fetus as token offerings for good luck.

"Now you place your offerings into our *despacho*. What are your intentions? What powers do you want from the gods? What are you going to do for the gods in return?" Rufino questions me with kind firmness, as any mentor would. With great care and intention, I wind my colored ribbons around the llama fetus, and place the prized hard-boiled egg in the center. Rufino has taught me that when the hard-boiled egg explodes in the fire of the *despacho* ritual, it is the sign that the gods have heard our prayers.

My prayers ask the gods to show me the way to step more powerfully into my sacred obligations as a shaman—to look after the wellbeing of both man and Mother Nature—and that I may help others do the same. As we tie up the offerings on the *despacho* paper my heart speaks clearly that the Amazon is to be the part of Mother Nature that I am to especially tend to. May it be so.

I have learned over the years of apprenticeship, that the essence of "spirituality" is connection—connection with spirit, helping people, with stewarding nature—connecting beyond oneself. Spirituality is not about narcissistic navel-gazing or shaking a rattle, or simply prayer alone. Prayer is more than words, it is a way of life. Spirituality is not static, it is how we live a life of reverence and good actions. Spirituality that transforms us and all our relationships is about connection, reflection, and pro-action. Pro-action implies living out the insights we obtain through reflection and prayer. Prayer is to be lived out. Spiritual insights motivate us, and demand that we take action. Otherwise, we're just catatonically sitting by the fire, not using our fire as a player and a practitioner of spiritual and worldly transformation.

I can hear my Amazon *maestro* saying to me, "Now we must get 'divorced'. That's what happens when the student becomes a full-fledged shaman. The student and the *maestro* must part ways." Afraid of losing him and my connection to him, he reassures, "I will meet up with you from time to time, don't worry. I will continue to come to you in your dreams, to guide and teach you. I will continue to send Spirit Doctors and Spirit Teachers to you in the form of spirits and in the form of people. Some of them will 'test' you and some of them will 'teach' you. It's up to you now to figure out how to navigate the world of spirits—both good and bad—for yourself. You are in charge of managing your own energy. You are now responsible for your own path, your own work in the world as a shamana."

"Remember, the power of a shaman is known by their work in the world. Power by itself is nothing, it's what you do with it that is important," my *maestro* instructs. He then looks down, turns, and walks away.

My own work in the world, yes.

I recall that Mary Oliver, Pulitzer Prize winning poet, once said in an interview, "My work is loving the world." As a famous and indefatigable guide to the natural world, she added, "Loving the world means giving it attention, which draws one to devotion, which means one is concerned with its condition, how it is being treated." In Oliver's case, her poetry is her power and work in the world. We all have a power and a work in the world.

I have a wish that we all step into our power, whatever that god-given magic that we each possess may be. Our power is our work in the world, our living prayer. The world needs each and every one of us to "be the medicine" for each other, and the world around us. May it be so.

21
The Wild Feminine

Greek mythology reports a sect of armed power-ful women named "Amazons" supposedly lived in the area north of the Black Sea. According to myth, the Amazons were an all-female society of fierce warriors. Over time, Amazons became an important theme in Greek, Hellenistic, and Roman art, and in subsequent cultural currents throughout history. This story goes that Spanish explorers named the great river of South America the "Amazon" because they believed that its territory also held the home of the myth-ical women warriors they heard about.

A local artist named Ricardo and I are enjoying a cup of coffee together in the Mitos y Cubietos Café, around the corner from the Victoria Regia Hotel and not far from the Plaza del Armas in central Iquitos. Mornings are the best time for hot coffee, before the equatorial tropical heat sets in for the day. Coffee shops are always the best place to meet up with old friends, or meet new ones—it's a great pastime in Iquitos. Richardo begins telling me that "the Muse of the Amazon is the Wild Feminine." As he sips his hot Nescafé instant coffee drink, ever so popular here in Iquitos, I ask the waitress if she would please make me a fresh-brewed *café con leche,* much more to my liking.

A few sips of my fresh morning coffee awaken me to the clarity and intent of his voice. Ricardo points to the many pieces of photography and local art hanging on the Café wall, and continues.

"For example, look at the all-green canvases over there, with the six green tree trunks each being hugged by several naked spirit women. What do you see?" he inquires.

"The tall jungle trees are covered with lots of tentacles of the Estrangulador Fig," I reply.

Ricardo adds, "This Estrangulador Fig, a member of the Ficus vine family, is an opportunistic vine that grows on trees due to the intense competition for sunlight deep under the canopy. I'm told that spiritually it represents the entwinement of love. The spirit women, symbols of the Estrangulador Fig vine, are hugging the forest trees—representing Love and Life itself."

"There is more," says Ricardo. "Now scan quickly all the other paintings, just to get the central themes. Tell me, what's your general impression of most, if not all, of these paintings you see?"

"I see women angels overlooking the forest with love and caring," I reply. "In that piece I see leaves of medicinal plants, each with a woman's head on top of the leaf. In this one I see a mosaic of leaves that come together to form a woman coming out of the jungle."

"Now, look at this photograph of the riverbank's edge of a primary jungle forest. What's your first impression?" Ricardo asks.

I answer, "I see bromeliads fanning out upon tree trunks, lianas draping off tree branches, and leafy vines trailing up tree trunks. I see the fecundity of life, upon life, upon life."

Ricardo pushes back his wooden chair, chair legs scraping the old blue *fleur-de-lis* ceramic floor tiles, probably left from the Rubber Barron days of Iquitos. Lifting his right arm and hand, turning his head to the right, he points his right index finger at the painting that is hidden behind him. He stands, and with that same right index finger, he outlines the prominent womanly figure, as if his finger were his paintbrush.

'The title of this painting is *Amazonia*," Ricardo begins. "The trees—her hair. The tree blossoms and tropical birds—flowers and barrette ornaments in her hair. The branches—her arms," he says, waving and circling his paintbrush-finger.

With even more energetic and generous strokes, his finger brushes the river tributaries, he adds, "Her pulsing flowing liquid blue river blood." He smiles.

And, to punctuate his art lesson, adds, "Yes, this is my painting. It's titled *Amazonia*, because I painted it with the idea that Amazonia is the Wild Feminine herself." He sits down across from me at the same table.

The naturally sensitive artist within Ricardo comes forth to speak. He leans forward, both elbows on the wooden table, hands clasped. Looking me directly in the eyes, his deeper self concludes the art lesson, "The Nature aspects of the Amazon call forth the nurturing, healing and life-giving feminine within. What happens when we're in the deep Nature of the Amazon is fundamentally about a calling forth of the Feminine in the human psyche that has been so dominated by the power-driven aspects of the Masculine in our modern lives." Ricardo impresses me with the depth of his art and what it means to him.

As he excuses himself for another appointment, I ask for a second cup of coffee. As I sip, I contemplate our brief and meaningful conversation. The steam from the hot fresh cup of coffee rises before my eyes. In this reverie moment, I recall somewhere reading about the possible origins of the word "Amazon" itself.

The name Amazon is said to arise from the Amazon Warrior Woman Myth. One accounting suggests that this cult of fierce and independent warrior women of the Amazon region had purposefully removed one of their breasts, so that they could pull back their bow and arrow more easily across their chest to become better huntresses. Their other breast remained intact to suckle their young. In fact, the name "Amazon" may have originated as "a-mazon" or "a = *without*" plus "mazon = *breast*". Seeing shirtless indigenous young men clad in grass-skirt-type coverings as they were pulling back their bows and arrows, the invading Spaniards might have thought they were women.

As all myths go, there are many versions. But the crux of the myth allows us to visualize these Amazon Warrior Women as the embodiment of the Wild Feminine that we call the Amazon—at once enormously untamed and immensely rich. I believe that Nature Herself is that Wild Divine Feminine, the breast from which we suckle life itself.

The wilderness and the wild feminine are both endangered species. We are in a cycle of experience where the pristine wilderness of our planet is disappearing, and the understanding of the wild feminine principle fades. Is it not surprising that many people view old women and old forests as unimportant?

22
Sacred Amazon

My best friends, Maia and Gil, are visiting me in the Amazon—a most delightful couple. They are engaged to be married soon back home in California. I can't wait to introduce them my *maestro*—I'm hoping he'll give them a special blessing. In fact, my *maestro* offers to do more than give them a blessing, he offers to give them a spiritual wedding ceremony deep in the Amazon forest, in a most auspicious spot. I'm to be her bridesmaid.

The water level of the Amazon River is high, which allows our *rápido* to take many smaller tributary short-cuts to get to the lodge in less time. I'm not sure it's all that much shorter of a trip, but it is pleasant to boat through pristine parts of the jungle with wildlife that is usually not seen.

The lodge staff greets us with open arms and thirst-quenching glasses of chilled pineapple juice. We're all spiritual family after all these years. My *maestro* rushes off the boat first, sure-footedly climbing over rows of seats in the rocking boat. He quickly disappears into the lodge while the staff helps us out of the boat to our accommodations and wrangles all our luggage after us. As we open the doors to our rooms, Maia and Gil are surprised and awed at the sight of a red heliconia-filled vase of flowers on the stand next to their bed. My *maestro,* who dashed ahead to get to their room first, thoughtfully left a special marriage-bouquet of jungle flowers.

Early the next morning, long before breakfast, my *maestro* disappeared into the jungle before we've had a chance to wish him *buenos días.* Never mind, I think to myself, I'm hungry and already on my way to the dining room for a plate of fried plantains, succulent watermelon, and fresh countryside *huevos t*he color of gold. Just as we're finishing my last cup of *té puro* after a delicious jungle breakfast, my *maestro* saunters into the dining room in time for his own breakfast.

"I've found a spot *muy perfecto* deep in the jungle for your wedding ceremony tomorrow," my *maestro* beams. "This afternoon I will prepare the area and make the other ritual items. Your marriage ritual will be tomorrow at 10:30am."

At 10:30am the next morning, with Maia and Gil clad in makeshift wedding garb, we excitedly leave the lodge in single file down the long path deep into the jungle to the site of the ceremony. We are also wearing knee-high rubber boots beneath our impromptu wedding clothes, a motley sight to see, as the jungle trail ahead is filled with many low-water spots and the ever-present possibility of snakes.

We are all hiking the trail—single file—deep into the jungle. The jungle is both the beauty and the beast. One minute, the threat of poisonous snakes, scary tarantulas, and the thought of getting lost on the jungle trail is enough to stimulate one's fear. The next minute the beauty of the jungle's flora and fauna is overwhelming—a breathtaking spotted mother ocelot rushing her two blue-eyed cubs to safety after spotting us humans. Two zany toucans overhead have a loud Lucy-and-Ethel conversation amongst themselves, and a plethora of beauteous lobster-clawed red-orange-green heliconia plants swing in the air beside us.

Always interested in the medicinal plant aspects of the jungle, I ask my *maestro,* "What is the 'medicine' of the heliconia plant?"

He turns and replies through a big smile, "The medicine of the heliconia plant is to bring beauty to the forest." As I smile back at his reply, he adds, "The spiritual uses of plants are as important as the physical medicines of plants."

That's my *maestro,* I muse, living in the poetry as well as the physicality of the universe around him.

After almost an hour of hiking in the brown muddy sludge of our trail—often almost stepping out of our rubber boots that get stuck in the muck—there is a turn in the jungle path that directs us to step on an amazing palm-frond-laden green wedding aisle that my *maestro* has prepared for my friends. I look up from the green-wedding-aisle jungle floor to see overhead an archway made of palm fronds braided together at the top of palm trees to mark the entrance to the jungle "chapel". As we step through nature's archway, we are each bestowed with a necklace of fresh red heliconia flowers and a freshly woven palm-frond *corona* (crown). On the other side of the archway, we find ourselves in a clearing surrounded by a ring of trees—a holy jungle chapel.

My *maestro's* ceremony sanctifies Maia and Gil's spiritual jungle marriage. His holy blessing puts all of us into a natural altered state of heavenly bliss. It is now that I realize he is invoking all the powers of his lineage and all the powers of the natural forces of the Amazon jungle to bless this Holy Union. Ecstatic waves of spirited energy coarse through my body. I am hit, once again, with the experience of the sacredness of the Amazon jungle.

We often think of Sacred Places and Sacred Sites as being filled with churches or sacred ruins—Mecca, the Vatican, Stonehenge, Machu Picchu. We may think a visit to the Amazon jungle—inherently not filled with churches or stony ruins—is not a sacred trek, that the Amazon jungles themselves are not sacred. I've learned differently. My *maestro* does not have a sacred holy altar upon a table, for he calls upon the spirit of the grand *living altar* that surrounds him. Flying macaws are sacred, the lively dolphins are sacred, the living plants and trees are sacred. He teaches me, "Sacredness—spirit—is without regard to form, the sacredness of Nature is everywhere."

What makes a place sacred—holy, hallowed, blessed, sanctified, venerated, or revered? I believe that whether a sacred place is manmade or a natural environment, it is human activity that consecrates a place and makes it sacred. If we invoke the spirit of the heavens, the earth, the water, the flora and fauna to bless our human lives, then it becomes a sacred activity in a sacred place. The powers of the Amazon are enormous. The spirit of the Amazon is enormous. The blessings bestowed by the Amazon are enormous. The sacredness of the Amazon is enormous.

I believe that when you come to the Amazon and experience this sacredness for yourself you will then know that the Living Amazon itself is the Sacred Amazon.

23
Voices of the Amazonians

These collected stories in this book are largely about what the Amazon means to me, what I have learned from my *maestro,* what other visitors to the Amazon think about the Amazon, and what scientists and experts know about the Amazon. Other voices of the Amazon echo in the many stories told to me by the local Amazonians themselves. What do they know in their bones about the Amazon? What in their experienced opinion is necessary to sustain the Amazon and its inhabitants? What are their visions, dreams, and hopes for this wild and unique place on Earth they call home?

It's 2pm, lunchtime in Iquitos. I'm on a hunt for some good Amazon stories, and lunchtime in the various *cevicherías* around Iquitos is a good place to find friends I can interview. Through the open door of one of many no-name *cevichería*, I spy Leo sitting alone. Leo is a local Loretano guide who speaks English—perfect! If I offer to buy his lunch, he is sure to give me the extra time I need to interview him.

Leo's eyes light up when I approach him with the offer of lunch. Soon we are munching on *langostinos*, prawns, and deep into conversation about what's needed for the Amazon to sustain itself.

"Young people here from Iquitos should visit the jungle," he responds quickly and easily. "They have little to no idea where they came from."

When I ask Leo to explain his comment further, he begins to unfold a singular story.

"My thirteen-year-old daughter, Carmen, was given a homework assignment on the topic of what her father does for a living. She wrote, 'My father is a jungle guide. He takes people from all over the world into the jungle.'"

"Upon reading her ordinary report, I said to my daughter, 'No. What you need to write about is the village where I'm from, where your grandparents are from. Did you know that my grandfather—your great-grandfather—was a chief and shaman of the Yagua indigenous tribe? I was actually born in this Yagua community, just up the river from here. This is the story of who we are that you should report on, not what we do for a living.'"

"I was present at her school the next day, as my daughter gave her report. I sat in the back of the room and listened proudly," Leo said with a big grin.

Leo then tells me in great detail about his daughter's report about the Yaguas.

"Today, the Yaguas live in some 30 communities scattered throughout the Peruvian and Columbian Amazon basin. The reason for the geographic dispersion, is due largely to the effects of the 'rubber boom' in the late 19th and early 20th centuries. At that time, Europeans arrived and began to exploit the indigenous people to extract natural latex from the jungle. Many Yaguas died in conflicts with the Europeans, as well as by exposure to European diseases. Others were exploited as slave labor. Ever since the rubber boom, sadly, the Yagua sense of unity and of common culture has declined," reported Carmen to her class. Leo comments to me that Carmen's report absolutely mesmerized the other students.

"The name 'Yagua' may have come from a Quechua term meaning 'the color of blood'. This term could have originated because of the red dye of the *achiote* fruit that they often paint on their faces. There is also another Quechua term that means 'royal palm', which could have easily referred to the palm fiber grass skirts that Yagua men wear," continued Carmen.

Carmen then showed her fellow students a Yagua blow-gun, as the Yaguas are a hunter tribe. She explained how the Yagua hunter, upon spying a monkey or sloth, takes a dart from a quiver, dips the tip into poisonous resin, and then carefully inserts the dart into his blow-gun. "These darts are tipped with paralyzing chemicals made from the rainforest plant known as *curare*. This is the principle of how early modern anaesthesia medicine came to use minute doses of *curare* in surgical suites to relax the muscles of the patients undergoing surgery," Carmen concluded.

At the end of the report, the teacher asked if Carmen's father was in the audience and would he please stand up. Leo tells me he stood up, as asked, not knowing what was to come. Then the teacher asked Carmen and her father to speak Yagua to each other, so the other students could hear a bit of the Yagua language. As they spoke

Yagua, the students' attention became electric. "The class applauded," Leo tells me with pride.

Leo reflects on his daughter's story with an understanding of its essential impact, "By interviewing me about her family's indigenous history, my daughter got in touch with her culture and her language. She appreciated me as her father, and where she comes from, in a bigger, more profound way."

Leo continues to explain that he then asked the members of the class if they ever visited the jungle where they are originally from. He recounts, "Most second and third generation students in his daughter's classroom had not had the opportunity to visit the jungle at all, much less visit the jungle place of their ancestry." Proud papa Leo added, "Her classmates got more interested in their heritage, and later found out another teacher at the school also spoke Yagua."

Leo is visibly emotionally taken by his own story. Shaking his head, Leo says, "Too much TV, Internet, and cellphones these days. It's all the younger generation are interested in. They are losing the richness and the wisdom of their indigenous jungle heritage. We need both the past and the present to move forward as citizens of the Amazon."

His daughter won a laptop computer for her spirited report. Her father won her deep respect.

Eduardo, a biologist at the Instituto de Investigación de la Amazonía Peruana (IIAP), agrees to meet me for tea at a café in IIAP. IIAP is a well-respected science and technological research institution specializing in the sustainable use of biological diversity in the Amazon region. We are nearing the end of our tea and lengthy discussion of the many factual reasons to conserve the flora and fauna of the Amazon.

Eduardo summarizes his opinion with a passionate personal plea, "We need to honor and conserve all that is the wilderness of the Amazon because people will want to know what those wild places were like when there are no more wild places. Wilderness and wild things not a luxury but a necessity of the human spirit." Shaking his head, he adds, "If we don't preserve and conserve, there will be no more wild places—there will be no more Amazon! There will only be national parks and reserves that will be merely stagnant 'nature zoos' of animals and plants." Eduardo downs the last of his cooling coffee and concludes, "Some people think you just put a fence around an area, and it's preserved, and that's all you need. They forget that a wild forest is a dynamic thing. We absolutely need the wildness—wild animals, and plants that grow wild. I worry that there simply will not be those wild places that are an absolute requisite to feed the wilds of our spirit."

Eduardo's comments remind me of the time when I took my *maestro* to the famous New York Botanical Garden, his first visit to the United States. Upon entering the Tropical Rainforest exhibit and seeing some of his favorite Amazon trees and plants in the conservatory, my *maestro* suddenly waves his hands and shouts, "These trees are stunted—they live in cages! What are you people doing? They need to be free to grow tall—this one here is 3 stories tall in the forest, that tree there normally grows 10 stories tall." Upon seeing the shocked expressions on my face and those of other visitors, he toned down his voice and added, "I do see that you water these trees well—but this is not letting these trees live, my friends."

I purposefully seek out Carlos, a good friend whose opinions I value, to get his thoughts on what the Amazon needs. Carlos, a successful Iquitos businessman with great respect for the Amazon, begins by sharing his perspective on growing up in Iquitos, and the town's relationship to its own historical roots in the jungle.

"*Motokars* only came to Iquitos when I was about twelve years old. Until then, you walked everywhere—to your friends, the market, and to the countryside. Where currently our family Iquitos business building stands today, there used to be a huge mango tree. As a boy, I used to pluck many juicy mango every day. I would eat one mango, then pick another, and eat another. The delicious juice of the mangos would run down my chin. I loved to eat mangos. It is one of my fondest memories of my childhood. I loved growing up in Iquitos.

"But now it is nature versus commercialism. There are too many *motokars*, too much noise, too much focus on money and materialism in Iquitos today," Carlos adds with a grimace. "The modern governments, too, in Iquitos and Lima primary focus is about the money. They should be governing from a higher ethical, moral, and ecological consciousness."

"The same is true with the thinking of the modern jungle people," Carlos continues. "They are largely focused on material goods, coming to the big city of Iquitos, making a living by selling something. They forget where they live—they forget the wealth of nature that surrounds them.

They do not know about conservancy and sustainability. All they want to do is to sell their jungle trees—maybe 80 *soles* (about $25) for a 100-year-old tree for a profit. The jungle people need education on the importance of the flora and fauna around them, and on how to make a living in other ways than selling the precious nature around them for a price. They need some guidance, so let's find ways to do that for them."

Carlos's eyes light up, as he shifts the focus of his comments. "The young people want to make a difference. They see what is wrong and what's to be done. Right now there is no money, no support by government, and no opportunity to make the changes that need to happen. Young people are the key."

"We must focus on the young people, the next generation," he concludes. "They can do it and will do it, because they already have the shift of consciousness necessary to move forward. We can shift from disorganization, lack of infrastructure, corruption, and materialism.

Let's find ways to support the young people in their efforts!"

Valeria, a dedicated scholar (a Master in Dogmatic Theology, and also Master in Conflict Resolution), states boldly, "Do you really want to know what I have to say?!" She adjusts herself in her chair to sit more upright, and goes on, "I love Iquitos and the jungle. I was born and raised here in Iquitos. There are so very many aspects needed for sustainability in the Amazon. But these many aspects are not the main problem. The problem is that we don't know how to use our intellect, our consciousness, to make a better life." Shaking an index finger into the air, Valeria emphatically states, "Poverty of the mind—not poverty of the streets—is the primary problem."

"If you want me to list all the aspects needed to make the Amazon sustainable, it would take pages and pages. The primary ingredient needed is a change of mentality," Valeria says, tapping a finger at her temple.

"The change of consciousness needed is not only individual, but systemic—the government, educational system, banks, workers, families. For example, the children need to be educated at school about ecology and conservancy; their families at home should reflect the same thinking; the adults must vote for the government officials that support environmental sustainability; and the banks should look to fund financially sustainable efforts to preserve the natural resources of the Amazon. Everyone everywhere has a role to play."

"Everyone and every social system needs, first and foremost, a change of consciousness," she concludes with academic certainty.

Lula is a native Iquitos young woman, full of creativity and vision, now living in Lima. I ask her for her thoughts on what the Amazon needs.

"Yes there is a core of people here in Iquitos that believe in and support ecology, nature and sustainability," Lula begins. "But there is no support from larger Iquitos or the government. Young people often leave Iquitos, to study at a Lima university, such as I did, and stay there."

"Sadly," Lula continues, "Iquitos does not value my creative vision nor support it financially at this time."

When I asked Lula if Lima is the location to make a plea for the Amazon, she answers, "Lima is not the place to do it—its archetype is 'city'. Iquitos—whose archetype is "jungle"—is definitely the place to affect change, for sure. And it will be slooooow.

"The consciousness of the people must be raised before anything can be done. And it will be the young people who do it," Lula adds.

"Paciencia," Lula concludes, "Patience—it will be a slow process, but worth it."

Born and schooled in Iquitos, Douglas now lives and works in Lima as an accountant. When I ask him what the Amazon needs to be sustainable, he becomes lit and animated. "People need to identify themselves more with their own region of the Amazon where they grew up or live now," he answers thoughtfully. "People destroy the jungle because they are separate from the jungle. If the people identified themselves with the jungle, they would not destroy it."

Douglas recalls his childhood life in Iquitos. "I enjoyed the closeness of my family. There were no cellphones, so we just talked together amongst ourselves all the time. I remember feeling so connected to my family and friends. I miss that closeness," he adds wistfully. "Then, when I was 22 years old, I went to work in the jungle. There, for the first time, I saw flocks of birds flying freely everywhere! I was amazed at a world of nature that I had no idea existed. I was astounded!"

"Then, like a lot of other Iquitos young people, I left Iquitos for Lima so that I could go to the University and then get a job there. Caught up in big city life in Lima, I forgot who I really was and where I came from." His eyes light up with realization as he adds, "Like so many other Loretanos, I forgot that we are the jungle."

"The world can live without humans, but we humans cannot live without the world around us," Douglas summarizes. "I now want to make a difference in the world, in the Amazon, and invite everyone else to join me," he concludes enthusiastically.

Another friend Tito, who is an Iquitos businessman and a philosopher by nature, remembers the easy nature-based aspects of Iquitos when he was growing up.

"What I remember most is swimming in the cool streams in the countryside near Iquitos. I loved this part of my youth," says Tito longingly.

"No malaria, no dengue fever, very few *moto-kars*. Life was simple, and it was about nearby nature experiences."

"I am now revisiting the pleasures of my childhood nature experiences. I regularly take my family, my wife and my sons, and a few friends to go to Santo Tomás, about 40 minutes outside Iquitos. There, we rent a houseboat to go out on a lake to swim and enjoy the nature surrounds. It's exhilarating and refreshing. We all love it, just as I did as a child."

"Now Iquitos is about commercialization, as is the psyche of this new generation. They want internet, cellphones, television, and to be part of the greater world around them," Tito continues. "But we must accept that all things change as the future rolls on—some things are perceived as *good* and some perceived as *bad* depending on the person."

Tito concludes, "Yes, sure, I like my air conditioning. And we don't want pollution from oil pipelines. But how do we move into our future—with all its material and energy needs—

and take care of the environment? This is *the* big question."

A gentleman, sitting at a table next to Tito and me, is quietly listening in on our conversation. I can tell he's eager to give me his differing opinion on the matter. I turn my chair around, introduce myself, and ask who he is and if he's like to add a comment to the discussion. From another opposing perspective, the only comment from this educated Iquitos businessman named Alfonso is, "I want my air-conditioning. The indigenous people, with all of their protests about the oil companies interfering with their welfare have to be made to understand this." And with that spiteful proclamation of belief, he returns to eating his now cold toast.

A local naturalist guide of the Yanamono village, north of Iquitos, is sharing his growing-up-in-the-jungle experiences with me. Fredy and I are enjoying an end of the day conversation together, sitting on a log bench overlooking the Amazon River at the peaceful Heliconia Lodge.

"I remember when my mother used to send me out into the planted fields to work, to tend to the *yuca* plants, bananas, and rice. 'Don't forget to check on the hens and chicks while you're at it,' my mother would shout at my back as I was already well down the jungle path," Fredy recollects. "Turning around to wave goodbye to her, she would add one more shout my way, 'And, Fredy, don't come home until the parakeet flocks fly overhead to roost.'" Reminiscing brings a twinkle to Fredy's eyes, as he comments, "We told time by the patterns of the birds and animals. We had no clocks or watches in the jungle. We got up in the morning with the sun, and went to bed with the sunset. Life was simple and good—I miss that."

"Our food sources changed with the rising and lowering of the Amazon River," Fredy continues as he taps more deeply into the memories of his early years in the jungle. "Each year, the Amazon rises and lowers some 6 to 12 meters. When the water is high, the animals naturally move to high-ground so that it is easier to find them and kill them for food—we ate lots of venison stew in high-water season. It is more difficult to catch fish in high-water because they are more dispersed. Conversely, when the water is low, fish are more concentrated, so fishing is easier—I love *pongo* fish soup! And during low water, the animals can roam around more freely in the extra land, so it is harder to hunt them for food. There is always food, just different kinds at different times of the year," Fredy reflects, pointing out to the lower river waters this July day. He makes a deep sigh, and makes a heartfelt summation, "I love the rhythms of the jungle life in the Amazon—all so natural and easy."

"What's missing, what's needed for the continued appreciation and sustainability of the

Amazon?" I ask Fredy, pulling him from his jungle life-review into the present.

"I truly believe that we have lost the oneness of all of life—including ourselves," he states knowingly. "As for me, that's why I have chosen the life of a naturalist guide—so I will never forget."

The simplest, yet profound, response to my queries came from my *maestro*. He was on a visit to my home in the San Francisco Bay Area, when he was asked by a young girl, "Now that you've been in the United States for several weeks, do you like the U.S.A. or the Amazon better?"

I awaited his response with bated breath. What, ultimately, is the value of the Amazon to this wise man?

My *maestro* paused for a moment, then answered thoughtfully, "Yes, it's true. I've had a wonderful time here in the U.S.A. And I hope to be able to come back some day. But, actually I 'feel better' when I'm in the jungle."

I, too, feel better when I am in the jungle.

24
Super Heroes
of the Amazon

This book really isn't about me and my jungle experiences—it's about you and your personal heart experiences that are evoked as you read it. A good storyteller does not just narrate details, but serves as an alchemist by taking details and making them a Great Story that touches the reader—that's you. Ultimately, what is your vision? What are your passions? Why are you here on this Earth? What has value and meaning for you in life—and what are you willing to do to defend and preserve it?

The Amazon serves as the muse for my passions and my work. My vision is that the Amazon will be the Garden of Eden that it once was at creation, and at the same time meet the needs of its modern people in a sustainable fashion. It is my hope that others will join in this vision of the Amazon—and if not the Amazon, that others will serve the bounteous Nature in their own back yards to the same end.

Some say the world is disenchanted. It is my belief and experience that ecstatic shamanic states can lift us to states of enchantment, charm and magic where everything is spirited and connected. This sense of connection helps us evolve from a mechanistic-reductionistic world-view to a systems world-view. The very heart of a systems world-view is in seeing the entire world as a network of inseparable patterns of relationships. A systems world-view gives us the opportunity to co-create our future together in right-relationship.

If you could, what would you do to help Mother Nature who birthed you and gave you life? What would you do to help Mankind who has helped you along the way? Some of you are already doing your passionate work, and others are still in the process of figuring it out for themselves. We are not called to "save the world", we are called to do our part in right-relationship with the world around us.

For those who are called to join us in the conservancy of the Amazon, I now dub you a "Super Hero of the Amazon". In my thinking, the word "conserve" means "con" = *with* and "serve" = *to serve*—so conserve, in essence, means *to serve with*.

Rachel Naomi Remen, M.D.—an oft-quoted spiritual teacher—reminds us, "Helping, fixing, and serving represent three different ways of seeing life. When you help, you see life as weak. When you fix, you see life as broken. When you serve, you see life as whole. Fixing and helping may be the work of the ego, and service the work of the soul."

How can we better *serve with* the people of the Amazon? You've heard their voices and their stories in the previous chapters. I believe the people of the Amazon themselves, the real Super Heroes of the Amazon, have the power to rectify the issues facing the Amazon today. Together, we can educate the public, and especially the youth, resulting in raising consciousness about local issues of the Amazon, respect for the flora and fauna of the Amazon, as well as major national issues affecting the Amazon River basin and its inhabitants.

Seeing is believing. Come. Come and experience for yourself the Eighth Wonder of the World—where flocks of colorful Dr. Seuss-ian long-beaked toucans fly overhead, so many that they seem photo-shopped! I welcome you to the jungle, the heart of an infinite green. Find a jungle path for the deepest encounter with nature—to get lost—and find yourself. Come to celebrate eternal sunshine and life-giving rain, where the locals celebrate life. The party is in the jungle—join us!

Start your journey in the city of Iquitos, often called the Capital of the Indigenous World. Named after the *Ikiitu* (Iquito) tribe, it is this ethnicity that has given the city of Iquitos its name. Iquitos is known as the "Amazon Venice" for its many waterways. Linked to the outside world only by air and by river, Iquitos is the world's largest city that cannot be reached by road. The city is surrounded on all sides by the Amazon, Nanay, and Itaya Rivers.

Within Iquitos, the district of Belén is known for its massive open-air street market and rustic stilt houses lining the Itaya River. The Plaza de Armas, in central Iquitos, is surrounded by charming European-tiled buildings dating to the region's early 20th-century rubber boom. Iquitos is a prosperous, vibrant jungle metropolis, along with the irresistible and exciting chaos of the rough edges of a jungle border town.

Iquitos—the Capital of the Amazon. This Peruvian port city is the Emerald Gateway to the jungles of the Amazon. The many spirited tales of the Amazon jungles that have captured your heart in these pages now call you to step through the dense green veil into another world.

Experiencing is knowing. Participate. Join in the circle of those who have experienced the magic of *la selva,* the jungle. We don't hold precious that which we don't know and love. Come and fall in love with Life itself.

Become a Super Hero of the Amazon, and help the Amazonians conserve the greatest expression of Life on Earth. Remember what my *maestro* instructed, "Gaining power itself is not the end goal. It's what you do with your power that counts. Your power is known by your work in the world." This is where your paddle hits the river.

Once again, from the heart. It's my last day in the jungle. With a bit of extra time to spare before the boat leaves the lodge, I decide to walk deep into the jungle to give a silent prayer of gratitude before I leave. Coming upon a perfect little clearing where sunbeams stream through the trees, I sit on a fallen tree trunk to settle into my gratitude meditation. The energies of this private place are especially sweet, they easily lull me into oneness with my surrounds. I quickly lose track of time and space—I am elsewhere now.

Out of the softness of the edges of my perception appears a beautiful spirit woman. As her countenance becomes more clear, I can see she has a piece of paper in her hand—a letter. Her angelic blue-green eyes catch mine, and I am mesmerized. Looking me straight in the eye, she starts with prayer, "To Our Father who art in Heaven, and Our Mother who art in Earth."

Then she looks at the piece of paper. "Thank you," she begins. "Gratitude is the purest orchid that grows from the vine of your soul." Reading from the letter, "We have deep gratitude for all that you are and all that you do out of love."

Her eyes shift from the letter she is reading aloud to making eye contact again. "Love happens—and you heeded the call of the Amazon." This diaphanous Amazon spirit woman keeps on with her ecstatic reading, all of which is at times too much to take in. Poetry, sheer enchanting poetry.

Vaguely, in the back of my mind I begin to wonder why she is there, why she is reading the letter, and to whom is this mysterious letter written. "We thank you for listening when we speak," she explains, her voice is coming not from her mouth but directly from her heart. The spirit of the Amazon is speaking directly from her heart to mine.

I'm finally able to come out of this rapture for a moment, long enough to ask her directly, "For whom is this letter?" Her answer, "This letter is for you, my dear, from all of us nature spirits of the Amazon."

And I turn to say to all of you, likewise, dear readers—the Amazon speaks—this letter is for you, dear ones.

Dancing River Girl

She roams with joy!
She cries with pain!
Her flanks rise like waves
and give pleasure
to the good man,
the boat man,
the fisher man.
She gives fish to them all,
smiles as they stroke her
with paddles and propellers.

She rises up with the rain
and drops down with the sun.
She lifts us up and fills our hearts
reflecting the sun,
the moon, the stars.

She is alive and calling us,
River Siren, the swimmer
alive near our shores,
the swimmer, sinuous and sexy,
swinging her hips,
her breasts in full sway
with milk for us all.

She flows and flows.
We touch her surface
and marvel at the cool,
the slick love she shares,
with all of the fish,

the dolphins rising
and spinning reflections.

The river she comes down
from the mountains,
slips over the rocks
and splashes over falls,
the pools catch her
and send her on,
though longing to hold her,
to keep her,
she must move on.

Dancing River Girl arcs,
embraces you, your boat,
your life.
She gives you life
and you give her life too.

The beat of your heart
matches her waves,
the movement of her legs
lifts your bow
and you rise and fall
as you will.

The rain wets you,
makes you more like her,
and you slip under,
together, forever...
with Dancing River Girl!

Amazon Poet

Interview with Connie Grauds

MT: What do you mean when you refer to the Amazon as "the greatest expression of life on Earth"?

CG: When I first come to visit the Amazon, my immediate impression of the flourishing biota was that life grows upon life upon life upon life in the rainforest. The statistics that are presented in this book are but a mere representation of the staggering statistics of the number of different species found in the Amazon. The detailed facts and figures on the biodiversity of the Amazon gathered by the experts in the fields of biology, botany, and ecology are astounding—worth looking into for those who are science-oriented.

For those who are more spiritually-oriented, I like to compare the Amazon to one sense of the Garden of Eden as being the original untouched beautiful garden of life. Deep in the jungles of the Amazon, where life is largely untouched by modern mechanization of any sort, there is a remarkable sense of peace and bliss—pure ambrosia. Extremely heady—a Garden of Eden.

Bottom line for me, being both of science and spirit, the Amazon is the ultimate expression—and experience—of life on Earth.

MT: You talk about the Spirit of the Amazon. What is the Spirit of the Amazon? How to we invoke/evoke it for ourselves?

CG: In the story where spirit took me up the long stairs to the tall gates that I was afraid to open, upon finally pushing the heavy gates open I was greeted by all this gift of immense love from the Spirit of the Amazon. The Spirit of the Amazon is nature-based love-energy, that has invited me in, acknowledged me, empowered me to know my own power. The Spirit of the Amazon inspires what I do to support and preserve the Amazon, and urges me to share with others the passion I have for this remarkable place.

When I/we experience spirit, it's easy for me to question it, and for others to question when we tell about it. I needed to trust myself in what I was experiencing, and that's how it lives into the future, in part. The power is not in what I/you think, but in my/your reality of experience. It is from this experience, this reality, that I do my best to live—to believe, trust, and live in that which has been given me.

When you come to visit the Amazon, I encourage you to take silent walks in the jungle—to let the jungle speak to you. It is in this silence that the sights and sounds and smells of the animals, birds, fish, insects, and plants are all speaking to us—asking us to listen and learn. From your own experience of this Spirit of the Amazon, you will know your own truth for yourself. No one can take that away from you.

MT: In the end, after all these years, what is the greatest gift that your experiences in the Amazon have given you?

CG: The Amazon, and all that it is, has given me my greatest sense of self—I came Home to my-self. And I continue to remember who I am, even more deeply, every time I step through the Emerald Doors of the Forest. I know that I am truly one with this great panorama of life, each and every time I look out over the Amazon River to the vastness of life itself. For this, I am truly grateful.

MT: What do you mean by the expression "as goes the Amazon so do we all?"

CG: I've learned that the Amazon biome is 2 times the size of India, and is home to 10% of the world's known species—unrivalled in scale and complexity anywhere in the world. However, the vastness of the Amazon is no safegard against deforestation. Don't be fooled. Scientists say that over the past 50 years, 17% of the Amazon forest cover has been lost, taking with it innumerable plants and animals. The Amazon River accounts for 15% of the total water discharged by all rivers into the world's oceans. If there is oil slick in the Amazon, there will be oil slick in our oceans.

It doesn't take an expert scientist to figure out that we must conserve the great Amazon biome, first and foremost—save the Mother, and she will continue to provide for all of us. While the Amazon may seem far away from your hometown and your concerns, conservation of the Amazon is a priority for everyone—no matter where you live.

MT: You call for consciousness-raising to happen as the next step in conserving the Amazon. How do you propose that to happen?

CG: Each must speak for themselves. As for me, I call for the recognition and celebration of an

annual Amazon Earth Day to be celebrated in
Iquitos, Peru—and around the world. The original Earth Day, founded April 22, 1970, was a de-
fining statement that Americans understood and
were deeply concerned over the deterioration of
the environment and the dissipation of natural
resources. This remarkable raising of consciousness of American citizens almost 50 years ago,
has become our internationally celebrated Earth
Day. Now it's time to add a special focus on the
plights of the Amazon by celebrating Amazon
Earth Day.

Come and help us all celebrate the preservation
of the most essential natural sanctuary left on
Earth—the Amazon Rainforest. Scientists and
people of all walks of life agree, as goes the
Amazon, so goes the World. Join us for an
Amazon Earth Day Celebration—in Iquitos!

It's human nature to care for things that we
value, that we love. Come and "fall in love" with
the Amazon. From there, we are all compelled to
tend to and care for what has value and meaning.

For those interested in coming together to organize and plan, and actualize the First Amazon
Earth Day to be celebrated here in Iquitos, kindly
contact me at www.LivingAmazonPeru.org.
I welcome like-minded, like-hearted community
to gather.

MT: What is the big message that you'd like readers to get from reading Amazon Speaks?

CG: Everyone needs to be responsible—that's the missing piece—for nature everywhere on the planet, not just the Amazon.

As for me—apparently a slow learner—I needed to be immersed into the immense power of the mighty Amazon and the sensate overwhelm of all of its green energy in order for me to get it. To use a medical term, I needed a full bolus—a big concentrated dose—of strong medicine in order to feel its effects. That's what my apprenticeship was about—feeling and tapping into the power around me and under my feet.

Now that I have my truth—my experience—of the power of nature in my mind/body/spirit, I invite each and every one of you to come to the Amazon to experience your own truth for yourself. You do not have to apprentice to tap into the medicine of the Amazon—it's in the sights and sounds and smells everywhere.

MT: You mention the shaman, your maestro, throughout the book. What are the gifts that he has given you over the years?

CG: Many of the gifts, the teachings, that my *maestro* has given me are recounted in my book *Jungle Medicine...from medicine to magic.*

To sum up here, the *aha* for my my scientific Western Medicine-trained mind was the extent and power of the "unseen world"—the world of spirit.

The revelation to me that my *maestro* can " see things" in a person's body and psyche that Western Medicine uses very expensive equipment to find. He doctors people both physically with herbs, and spiritually with forces of the unseen world. As strange or unbelievable as these things seem to be as a western-trained pharmacist, I saw him repeatedly demonstrate that to be true. It opened my mind to the possibility of health evaluation and healing happening in a spiritual way, that I can't explain in a scientific way, but that I have come to believe in my experience.

The big gift from my *maestro* is my own personal empowerment. My apprenticeship can be summarized by stating that it empowered me by opening me up to the "best me" possible. It has maximized my capacity—intellectually, intuitively, energetically. As my *maestro* said to me, "The purpose of your apprenticeship is to potentize you." And, as he added, 'The power of a shaman is known by their work in the world— prayer in action. So get on with it!"

About the Author

We all must become the medicine the world needs. Now is the time.

Shamans have, in their practices and principles, always been healers of the sick and keepers of the forest. Their responsibilities are to look after the wellbeing of both Mankind and Mother Nature.

The power of a shaman is known by their work in the world. To that end, as needs arise for appropriate action to assist humankind and in conscious stewardship of nature, all shamans and supporters of shamanic principles are called to act on behalf of Mankind and Mother Nature.

The mighty Amazon is the greatest expression of life on Earth. As goes the Amazon, so goes the Earth. Take the river of personal empowerment with Connie—become the medicine the world needs.

Connie Grauds, RPh, MNPA
www.ConnieGrauds.com

www.ingramcontent.com/pod-product-compliance
Lightning Source LLC
Chambersburg PA
CBHW031246090426
42742CB00007B/329